TRIUMPH IN TURMOIL:

HOW I EMBRACED MY ADHD SUPERPOWERS TO GAME THE SYSTEM

BY
KELLY E. MIDDLETON

EDITED BY
MIKE MAVILIA ROCHESTER

Triumph in Turmoil: How I Embraced My ADHD Superpowers to Game the System

Pulished by Kelly E. Middleton
30 W. 8th Street
Newport, KY 41071
www.kellymiddleton.com

Edited by Mike Mavilia Rochester
Proofreader Michael Fedison
Layout by Sophie Hanks
Cover Design by Arash Jahani

ISBN: (paperback) 978-1-7374608-2-4
ISBN: (ebook) 978-1-7374608-3-1
Library of Congress Control Number: 2024912593

TABLE OF CONTENTS

PREFACE

ADHD is one of the most common disorders among children, with six million children diagnosed and over nine million adults diagnosed in the U.S. alone. [1,2] It is a widely researched and treated diagnosis, and yet, many of us with ADHD struggle to thrive in the world. This book aims to shine some light on many of the ways those of us with ADHD can excel in life by viewing our ADHD as a tool for success instead of a disorder that needs to be treated and suppressed.

Growing up with ADHD, in a time when even the term *attention deficit hyperactive disorder* had not been invented yet, I always knew I was "different" than other kids. I had to overcome obstacles my peers did not experience just to make friends, navigate the dating world, and even graduate from school.

I've spent over thirty years working with students and staff with ADHD as a public school teacher and administrator.

As a parent of kids with ADHD, I've experienced the challenges of watching my children struggle with aspects of life that many kids without ADHD take for granted. There's nothing like getting your kid ready for school only to hear them exhale in frustration when they realize they forgot to do their science fair project, due in only a few short hours. But that's just part of life with kids who have ADHD. I will say it helped me that I could at least *relate* to them in these moments!

My goal in writing this book is to make people feel better about their ADHD. So much of the literature and discussion focuses on the *illness* aspect of ADHD and not enough on the positive side of ADHD. We are being asked to conform to the point where our gifts are not appreciated; in fact, they are often suppressed. This book celebrates our uniqueness by highlighting our ADHD superpowers and gives examples of how I have used them to accomplish my goals and live a full, happy life.

INTRODUCTION

"Birds born in a cage think flying is an illness."

—Alejandro Jodorowsky[3]

My name is Kelly Middleton, and I am a retired public school superintendent with thirty-two years of experience in education. Like many people with ADHD, I suspected I had it for many years before being diagnosed—at the age of fifty. Throughout my childhood, I unknowingly developed different methods to cope with my ADHD tendencies and harness my ADHD talents. You'll find my methods and stories throughout this book. As a schoolteacher, principal, coach, superintendent, writer, and presenter, I have a plethora of both personal and professional experiences to draw upon that can help those of us with ADHD succeed in today's world.

Having ADHD can be debilitating for many of us. Most schools and many professions are just not designed for people like us. The lack of education on ADHD can even make personal relationships extremely difficult. However, if you know your ADHD superpowers and learn how to *game the system* you can not only adapt to the demands of today's society, but you can also flourish and become extremely successful in whatever you choose to do. I'm proud to say that by knowing my gifts and strengths, I now have the confidence to take on any life challenge. I believe so much in my superpowers that there are times when it almost seems unfair to those who do not have the gifts that come with ADHD.

I don't believe I am "deficient" with attention. I prefer to say I'm attention selective. In other words, I might give my attention to *only* people and subjects that truly interest me. Allow me to get hyperfocused on a task and let's see someone without ADHD give the task *more* attention. **I do not believe ADHD is a disorder. Everyone with a true disorder more than likely would gladly get rid of it.** My children and I, along with my numerous ADHD friends and many great athletes, actors, and other highly successful individuals, would never give up our ADHD superpowers. If a cure was developed for ADHD, my children and I would pass on this opportunity. Giving up our superpowers would be the equivalent of Superman giving up his strength or ability to fly or Spider-Man willingly losing his ability to cast a web.

Before I discovered my ADHD superpowers, people thought I was a little slow and maybe not all that smart because all they could see were my ADHD symptoms. People shortchanged me and judged me before they really knew me, which caused me to develop a chip on my shoulder. I always felt like I had to prove myself to others. I may be scatterbrained at times, but that doesn't mean I can't think deeply or critically. Sure, I still make a lot of mistakes— when I hear something break, I immediately wonder if it was my fault. Sometimes it is even refreshing to me when others make mistakes so I can proudly proclaim, "It wasn't my fault!" That is why it is important for people to know why I think like this. When others make mistakes, it just makes me feel more normal. Much like Popeye opening his can of spinach, those of us with ADHD should have our superpowers on hand and ready to use when life gets challenging.

Full disclosure: I don't always feel "super." My ADHD sometimes gets me down, especially when I make dumb mistakes or get hurt doing everyday tasks. Those of us with ADHD might get mad or frustrated when this happens. It might also be hard for others to understand and they may take my anger personally. In reality, I am just mad at myself. However, I've learned humility from my mistakes and have learned to just stop and laugh at myself. I know I'm a better person because of my many ADHD faux pas.

Have You Ever . . .

Those of us with ADHD know that we have tendencies that many without ADHD do not have to struggle with each day. Recently, my wife and I were making sandwiches at our house. For me, bacon is a key ingredient in a sandwich. I put the bacon in the microwave and went to my plate to put the cold ingredients on my sandwich. Wouldn't you know, I forgot the bacon. I ate my sandwich and finished my day. In the middle of the night, I woke up and remembered the bacon and kicked myself for forgetting. I'd had the powerful smell of the bacon, the beeping of the microwave, the sight of the sandwich without the ends of the bacon poking out, and the taste of the sandwich without a key flavor—all to remind me about the bacon—and yet, it was not enough. Mistakes like this are common in my ADHD world. I've listed a few others below that you may be able to relate to. Have you ever . . .

- been looking for your glasses when they were on the top of your head?
- gone to the cabinet to get something and forgot what it was you were supposed to be getting?
- left your car running and forgot about it?
- bought something you did not need on an impulse?
- waited until the last minute to study or do a project even though you had plenty of time to complete it beforehand?

- daydreamed for extended periods of time?
- had trouble not interrupting others when they were talking?

These are just a few examples of my ADHD tendencies. If these examples strike a chord with you, this book may help you unlock your ADHD superpowers.

Communicating Our Idiosyncrasies Is Key

Most of the actions above are very common to those of us with ADHD. Hey, even Superman had his kryptonite. By knowing, embracing, and telling others about our tendencies, we can lessen the severity and frequency of these situations. For example, I know I tend to interrupt people when they are talking. However, if the person knows I have ADHD and I interrupt because I am very interested in the conversation, they know I am not being disrespectful. I just got excited and thus did not take time to self-talk myself into waiting my turn to speak. I also know that if I do not tell you what is on my mind right then, the thought may be lost forever. By explaining this to people up front, they have a better understanding when you do interrupt them in mid-sentence. Communicating our ADHD idiosyncrasies to others is one way to have better relationships in both your personal and professional life.

I Am Not a Doctor

I want to be very clear—I do not have a medical degree and do not want anyone to think I am giving any medical or professional advice. The stories and examples in this book are just my personal experience. Always talk with your doctor who knows your medical history. My experience comes from:

- Being undiagnosed for fifty years and developing coping mechanisms as needed
- Being diagnosed and starting medication at age fifty
- Having two children who were diagnosed with ADHD at an early age
- Mentoring and counseling students and adults with ADHD
- Being a school leader for many years, both taking and not taking ADHD medication
- Being a principal of a primary school, middle school, and high school for several years
- Working with students and parents as they struggled with making the decision to medicate or not
- Working with teachers, bus drivers, and support staff who worked with ADHD students each day
- Working with nurses and office personnel who had to regularly house and dispense ADHD medication each day

I have crafted these chapters partly from of my own experience, but also from my years of observing others with ADHD, including my children, students, and coworkers.

The Power of Self-Talk

I think of self-talk as a conversation with myself so I don't do something I will regret. Self-talk makes me aware of my impulses and is a way to slow down and check in about what I'm doing. It's like the window that pops up on your computer that asks, "Are you sure you want to do that?"

I started self-talking early on when I knew something was not right. I was making some stupid mistakes and was so frustrated about it that I started to remind myself to wait, sit still, listen, or keep trying.

If I'm cooking something on the stove, without fail, I'll want to do something else before I'm done cooking. So I have to tell myself, *Kelly, you better stay here and finish or you might burn your house down.* I can't stand being behind a slow car. I have to self-talk to ask what could be coming around that curve, or think if I pass this car I may die and I may not see my grandchildren graduate.

Sometimes, self-talk is about predicting what may happen and making a game plan for what I will do. At a board meeting, I will self-talk: *If X comes up, this is what I'm going to do or say.*

Using self-talk at the right times is key. On the other hand, if you're self-talking while someone is introducing themselves, you're going to miss their name.

Self-talk can be exhausting. One-on-one meetings, daily tasks, home life—all can be draining if you're self-talking during these. A shower, bath, or exercise can be a welcomed break for me. Alone time can be especially important on days when I'm feeling drained by self-talk.

One interesting discovery I found recently was how much drugs like Adderall can help. When I am on my medication, I find I do not need to self-talk as much, if at all. Since self-talk is about controlling impulses, and the Adderall takes those impulses away, the need to constantly self-talk goes away too. I don't take ADHD medication all the time. But when I do, life is easier. Every conversation is easier. Reading directions is easier. It is a trade-off though. I find I am also less interesting and fun. Self-talk is a way to get the benefits of ADHD medication without these drawbacks.

My Thoughts on Medication and Diagnoses

I first considered taking Adderall when I was fifty years old. I have a great family doctor who was wary of prescribing the medication, as he did not want to speed up my heart at my age. After all, my coping mechanisms seemed to be working and I was coming to the end of my career. After a long discussion, he finally agreed to give me Adderall with a lot of monitoring and supervision. The impact for me was amazing. I remember thinking, *Wow—is this how life is supposed to be?* Life became so much easier and all I could think about for a while was how I wish I'd had the medication when I was in school. I immediately became a better school leader, father, partner, etc. At my next doctor's visit, I told my doctor that if I die five years earlier than expected, due to the medication, it would still be worth it.

I've found that taking ADHD medication usually has some effect on my superpowers. It can either enhance or subdue each superpower. Knowing this, I've learned to carefully consider which situations I believe will benefit from medication and which I think I'm better off unmedicated.

After being diagnosed with ADHD, I began reading stories and books on ADHD and had so many aha moments. Oh, how I wished that I had been diagnosed and had access to this information earlier in life. Then I remembered, before medication, I was always aware I was different. That self-awareness allowed me to find the superpowers hidden in my limitations and harness them to my benefit. I was lucky that I found many ways to manage my ADHD, like playing sports as a kid and working in middle schools as an adult—environments in which my high energy was a benefit, not a detriment. Many with ADHD are not so lucky and end up turning to drugs or alcohol to cope or work jobs that don't fit with their unique skills and personalities. Maybe they don't finish school, frustrated knowing they are different without knowing why or how to make the most of their differences. Some are always trying to be like everyone else when they should be embracing who they are. We all need to get better about ADHD. We need to wear it like a badge of honor. Schools must get better at recognizing our tendencies and guiding us into our strengths rather than placing us in special needs classrooms. Hopefully, this book can bridge some gaps for everyone, whether you have ADHD, know someone with ADHD, or work in a field like education where you can help those with ADHD.

All of us remember the story of "Goldilocks and the Three Bears" where Goldilocks would try the porridge, chairs, and beds, inside the bears' house. Goldilocks would always find that those items that belonged to Baby Bear were just right. When it comes to ADHD medication, we should be like Goldilocks—always looking for the dosage, situations, and timing that is just right. Make no mistake, this is a moving target as we grow, as our bodies become used to the medication, and as we become more cognizant of the effects of the medication. It takes some work, but in my opinion, it is well worth it!

A few side effects of ADHD medication I have personally noticed:

- Medication will cause a person to lose their appetite.
- Medication is a stimulant that calms us down.
- Medication may make it hard to sleep.
- Medication may make it harder to have sex.
- If I take medication every day for a while and then stop cold turkey, I get very tired.

Positive outcomes I have personally noticed:

- I can concentrate at a much higher level.
- I will stay on task until a job is complete.
- I have greater courage and confidence in social settings.
- I am very calm.
- I do not interrupt people.

At times I am like Goldilocks looking for the Baby Bear dosage that fits me just right for the situation. When I was working in education, I usually took half my dosage through the week and did not take any on the weekends. In retirement, I only take medication as needed. Sometimes, I take it if I am writing, presenting, or reading. I may take it if I need to really concentrate hard on a task. I keep my medicine on me in case of emergency, like if I'm spinning out of control from my ADHD head chaos and need to calm down.

My Family and Background

My mother, Kandy, has always believed she had ADHD but never sought treatment. I was born in the '60s and ADHD was not widely understood or diagnosed. My son, Russ, and daughter, Erienne, were both diagnosed with ADHD at a young age. They are now in their thirties, college-educated, and have great jobs. They also still routinely take their ADHD medication. Both of my children embrace their ADHD, and while they would admit there have been struggles, they would never want to give up their ADHD superpowers.

I was married to my first wife, Mary, for over twenty years and she does not have ADHD. I often think about the trials of marriage and how she had to negotiate a husband and two children with ADHD. Mary and I are still good friends and often do things as a family along with my second wife, Amy. Mary and Amy like to bond over sharing crazy stories about my ADHD tendencies. It's like two army buddies talking about their battle scars from war.

Amy does not have ADHD, but has brothers who do, so she knew what she was getting into when we first started dating. We have such a great marriage because we talk about my strengths, superpowers, and areas I need to totally avoid and leave up to her. We divide up all our tasks and responsibilities based on each other's strengths. Without her knowledge of ADHD tendencies and my ability to self-talk and use my superpowers, our marriage, like so many other ADHD marriages, would be a disaster. I will discuss how we make it work throughout this book. I believe many of us with ADHD are naturally attracted to highly organized individuals without ADHD who will complement our scattered, thrill-seeking brains. At Amy's request, I try not to medicate as she tells me she likes the unmedicated me. She is all about having fun, and she tells me when I medicate, I am very focused, mistake-free, and less chatty. You'll find several of our stories in this book.

The Superpowers List

The chapters in this book are centered on the superpowers that I believe exist in individuals with ADHD. I did not pull this list out of thin air—most of these superpowers are described in ADHD literature. I tried my best to include every possible superpower I've experienced.

There are experts who are skeptical that such positive ADHD traits even exist. There are also children and adults who have never heard about the possibility of having these powers and thus do not know how to harness them. To me, it is as if they are walking around with Popeye's can of spinach but have no idea what is in the can.

I do not claim to possess every superpower, but I try to harness as many as I can in the name of self-improvement. The more I read and study, the better I become at gaming the system and unlocking more powers. For me, medication can be a hindrance with some of these powers and a tremendous help with others. It is my hope that everyone with ADHD and without ADHD (parents, guardians, teachers, family, and friends) can learn about these ADHD superpowers. For those who must deal with our ADHD behavior, relationships can be saved and improved, teachers can better reach students, and friendships can be strengthened. By learning to use your superpowers, you may end up saving your life, saving your marriage, keeping or excelling at your job, and fully enjoying life. I suggest you read and digest these superpowers one at a time. Reflect on each one and try to remember when and if you've seen or even used each power. I have provided stories from my life—not to brag, but to provide examples to help the reader see these superpowers within themselves or others who might have ADHD. My goal in writing this book is for those with ADHD to realize they are truly special. We should be proud of our ADHD and wear it like a badge of honor. I hope you can use this book to learn just like I did about each of these superpowers and practice using them until they are at your disposal at all times and in every situation.

One of the most shocking pieces of evidence I've found that shows it's hard to be a kid with ADHD came when I was speaking with ADHD expert Dr. Vincent J. Blanch, MD/PhD. He told me that students with ADHD who are not medicated must work four times harder in school than their peers. Is it any wonder students with ADHD have trouble in school and have high dropout rates? In the face of these massive educational challenges, students with ADHD who make it to graduation must demonstrate tremendous resilience. Not only would they have had to overcome the challenge of having to work harder, but they would also have had to bounce back when they did not meet their achievement goals. This is the heart of resiliency and one of the reasons why, in my own professional career, when I must fill a position, I'd gladly take the resilient, hardworking ADHD person who had to overcome all the issues we have had to face on a daily basis.

Resilience in My Personal Life

Car wrecks are quite common in our ADHD world. I had a major crash going into my sophomore year of high school. This wreck could have easily been the end of my basketball career. I broke many bones in my face, which required my jaw to be wired back together. Subsequently, I lost a lot of weight and a great deal of strength. This was before weight lifting was a major part of basketball training, so I had a lot of strengthening to do before anyone would ever consider recruiting me. I had a choice at that moment—to throw in the towel or to accept the challenge. I chose the latter, which meant putting in the work *every day*: learning to jump again, pushing myself when my shots were coming up ten feet short, and adding an extra set of sprints when I felt like I had nothing left in the tank. I was so far away from game shape over those long months of training, which really tested my resilience. At times, I didn't see how I would ever be able to rejoin the team.

Thankfully, I also had the ADHD chip on my shoulder from my notion that I was not quite as good as my peers. That desire to prove myself, plus my resiliency superpower, would get me back into playing shape in a short period of time. My resiliency superpower propelled me to being named first-team all-state in basketball—one of several athletic achievements I would earn through my tenacity and work ethic. More importantly, my resiliency afforded me athletic scholarships that paid for college, which would have never been possible without my ADHD superpower.

For those with ADHD who feel like they just cannot make it through the tough times, know this: you have something within you that will allow you to outwork others. Once a person combines the lessons learned from living with ADHD and their resiliency superpower, I truly believe they can be successful and overcome any life situation.

Sometimes our ADHD differences can make us feel like we don't match up with our non-ADHD peers, especially those of us who were told we would never amount to anything. Well, here's a list of people with ADHD who proved those naysayers wrong:

Emma Watson
Woody Harrelson
Justin Timberlake
Ryan Gosling
Michael Jordan
Carrie Underwood
Liv Tyler

These are just a few famous people with ADHD. I've sprinkled more (and their stories) throughout this book.

Resilience in My Professional Life

It is very important for those of us with ADHD to find a career where our superpowers can help us be successful as opposed to stifling us. Many people with ADHD are constantly changing jobs due to boredom or just making quick decisions to quit without giving it a lot of thought. School administration was a perfect fit for me. Being a school administrator, I was constantly inundated with paperwork and bureaucracy procedures. Each day, I had to make decisions for the school that were in the best interest of students while complying with school policy, board policy, bargaining contracts, and school law. Besides that, I had to keep up with the approximately fifty to one hundred *new* educational bills and laws that go through legislation each year in our state. It required a lot of resilience, cutting through all that red tape for the sake of the kids!

For many of my peers, this job is enough to make them want to quit or "quiet quit." That is, not put in the effort to make their school or district better by doing the bare minimum to not get fired. These constant issues take up all their energy and bandwidth. However, for me, my ADHD superpower kicked in and I got EXCITED about all the challenges in a school or district and so I just met them head-on. By making it a challenge, I was revving up my resilience superpower. I chose to stick my neck out, to face adversity and risk failure, in order to push my ideas for improvement and change in my schools, including new initiatives, renovating schools, building new schools, and closing old ones. Each day is always different in the world of school and district administration, which makes it an attractive job for my ADHD brain.

There's an old saying, "Ships in harbor are safe, but that's not what ships are built for." What are we doing in leadership if we are not working tirelessly against all opposition and failure to improve the experience of our customers? That's resilience.

Many of my initiatives as a school leader were uphill battles. My professional resilience was tested regularly at school board meetings, including an initiative called the Double Nickel Tax, which I'll explain in another chapter. During these difficult moments, I remember I've got my resilience superpower in my back pocket, so I'm not afraid of losing my job. If I ever get fired, I know I'll bounce back and get another job. My resilience made me not afraid of change or failure. I've found that failure and adversity are nothing more than fuel that ignites me to come back even stronger.

If you have ADHD and find yourself struggling at your job, ask yourself this one question: Am I in the right career field where I can utilize my ADHD superpowers? If not, consider the superpowers in this book before making your next career move.

Here are some of my ADHD attributes. These are the traits I would want others to know about me so they can understand how my ADHD manifests.

1. I drink a lot of coffee. It relaxes me.
2. I lose my keys, sunglasses, and cell phone on a regular basis.
3. I make a lot of mistakes when I am tired.
4. I secretly celebrate when you make a mistake because it was not my fault. It makes me feel more normal.
5. I will interrupt you because I am afraid I will forget my thought.
6. I eat impulsively.
7. I will take risks that others will not take.
8. I always feel like I am out of time and will try to cram as many activities in a day, or hour, as possible.
9. I will be so focused on other things that I may trip over something I should have seen.
10. I will not take time to read directions.
11. I procrastinate but will work harder to complete on time, even to an extreme.
12. I will stop working on a project just before I am about to finish the project.
13. I will do many tasks at the same time and leave them all uncompleted.

14. I leave groceries in the cart, forgetting to put them in the car.

15. I will walk into a room and forget why I went in there.

16. I will not remember your name, but that does not mean I do not care about you.

17. I get stressed in airports.

18. It is hard for me to concentrate on taking a test if there are any distractions.

19. I burn food by trying to cook it too fast or by trying to complete other jobs while cooking.

20. I will buy items on impulse. I need to wait a day on all decisions that have lasting impacts such as tattoos.

21. I can easily become hyperfocused on the wrong thing.

22. I have a chip on my shoulder to prove to people I am not stupid.

23. I read people and situations very well.

24. I am a great problem-solver and out-of-the-box thinker.

25. If you are competing against me, you do not want me to become hyperfocused on beating you.

26. I hate to be told to do something at the last minute. As the saying goes, "Lack of planning on your part does not constitute an emergency on my part."[4]

27. I need a morning routine.

28. I do not sleep well and may have a restless foot or leg.

29. I may get lost quite a bit while driving as my mind wanders. I will miss turns frequently unless I'm concentrating.

30. I may become very frustrated at myself—just give me a little space and do not take it personally.

31. I like to walk and think at the same time as I am a better problem-solver when moving.

32. When medicated, I do not even think about sex.

33. I only care about a class or subject in school or college if I become hyperfocused on it or if I connect with the teacher.

34. I make a mess when I eat.

35. I make a mess at the bathroom sink.

36. Sometimes I forget where I parked and will need to use the car alarm to find it.

37. I need to be careful when shopping so that I do not forget what I am doing and walk out with an item without thinking and then be accused of shoplifting.

A Few Tips on Resilience

Because of our resilience, many with ADHD have a hard time understanding others' lack of resilience. I can become frustrated easily when others quit something before they have given it a chance or refuse to even try to learn something new. I must constantly remind myself that others perhaps did not have my struggles early in life. Perhaps they had parents who allowed them to quit early and often when something was not going their way. By knowing our own tendencies, we can self-talk, when necessary, so we don't make others feel bad for not having our skills.

On the other hand, sticking with a difficult task can backfire. Sometimes our brains can get "stuck." What I mean is that we may have in our mind that a certain task needs to be completed and we cannot accept not finishing it. Stopping or giving up because it's really not worth the extra effort simply "does not compute." Below are some examples of this idea. Do any of these apply to you?

- We may stay with a task longer than we need to because we just do not want to quit.
- We may stay in a relationship that is not healthy for us much longer than we should.
- We may risk our reputation, job, or even safety on a task because we just refuse to give up.

There is an adage: "If you find yourself in a hole, stop digging." This could often apply to the ADHD brain. I can be doing a job or an activity and everyone else is ready to stop and I want to keep working. When leading a group of people, I must be conscious of knowing when everyone else has had enough. Self-talking and letting everyone know my ADHD tendencies helps me and others understand this superpower.

I realize that this is the opposite of how I mentioned earlier that those with ADHD might quit tasks early. This goes to show how ADHD can make us go to and live in the extremes.

Superpower 2

High Energy

Having high energy just goes with having ADHD. Imagine having all this energy and going to school only to be told to sit and be quiet on the school bus, in the classroom, during lunch, and on the bus ride home. If I act up, perhaps you take away the one thing I love . . . recess. Compound this with mandated homework and you have completely tortured my ADHD brain from dusk to dawn. It's no wonder so many children with ADHD resort to taking drugs to survive getting through the school day.

Hyperactivity is a trademark trait of ADHD. It's also seen so negatively that many with ADHD feel ashamed of their high energy and try to bottle it up. You may be sitting there wondering how having high energy could be a superpower. Keep reading to find out.

High Energy in My Personal Life

"My report card always said, 'Jim finishes first and then disrupts the other students.'"[5]

—Jim Carrey

I use this ADHD superpower each morning to clean the house, run errands, and have an active social life. I like to tell people how I channeled this superpower a couple of years ago with Amy. We had only been married about a year. Amy challenged me to run a 5K with her in a race they call "The Flying Pig" in Cincinnati. While I played multiple sports at the college level, I never considered myself much of a runner. Amy, on the other hand, is not an athlete, but enjoys running in 5K races. Now, I never liked to run and at age fifty-seven I did not want to start. I had never participated in any races before in my entire life. When we were training for this 5K, Amy beat me every time. I even pulled a hamstring during one of our early training sessions. Not only is Amy quite a bit younger than me, but I also was nowhere near the shape she was in! However, Amy *did* appreciate my effort and even felt bad for me when I injured myself. I remember one day riding in the car she was telling her mother about me running in the race. I heard her mother through the phone ask, "How *old* is he?" It was at that very moment I decided to call upon my high-energy superpower to secretly train while Amy was at work. If you recall from the last chapter, I have a chip on my shoulder and this was the motivation my ADHD brain needed to kick into gear and activate my superpower.

Finally, on the day of the race and while we were riding to the starting point, she turned to me and said sincerely, "I won't pull ahead of you. Let's just run together." I was so determined to surprise her, that extra motivation fueled me. I summoned my high-energy superpower, and sure enough, I left her in the dust. I beat her time by two minutes and twenty-seven seconds. I have the event poster framed with our bib numbers and times in the corners so she wouldn't ever forget. The poster hangs proudly in my man cave. This was the only time I had ever beaten her during our months of training. After the race I collapsed and could not walk for about two weeks. It was worth every bit of the pain. I tell this story to demonstrate how I can call upon my superpowers when needed.

Karina Smirnoff is a regular on *Dancing with the Stars* and has won dance championships all over the world. She says, "My parents tried anything and everything just to address my inattention and provide an outlet for my hyperactivity. They enrolled me in activities that held my interest like figure skating, ballet, gymnastics, and playing the piano." Between all the practice, choreography, travel, taping for shows, and teaching, she's in the right field to use her high-energy superpower.[6]

My high-energy superpower worked to my advantage in college. After growing up with very little money, I found I am motivated by having nice things and making a good paycheck. So, I learned to channel my energy to be successful. I attended Georgetown College on a basketball and tennis scholarship, taking eighteen hours each semester and additional classes each summer and by correspondence. I played two college sports and found time to have a job on campus. I graduated with my teaching degree, a bachelor of science degree, and a bachelor of arts degree along with a double minor. I went on to quickly get my master's and various school administrator certifications, allowing me the opportunity to be a school leader within eight years. In addition, I was also a two-time NAIA Academic All American in basketball and had great tennis success, eventually being elected to the Georgetown College Hall of Fame for both basketball and tennis. All this is not to toot my own horn, but to show that, when motivated, those of us with ADHD can activate our high-energy superpower to achieve our goals.

The other side of the coin is that I do not even remember college life. I have very few classmates with whom I am friends. I was not medicated and was stressed the entire time. To this day I have nightmares of forgetting about college classes or ball games. I remember college as a job and a means to an end and never can relate to others when they talk about how much fun they had during their college years.

I love to read about famous people with ADHD. Michael Jordan was arguably the greatest basketball player to ever play the game and has mentioned being diagnosed with ADHD. While he has tremendous natural athleticism, there might be better shooters and ball handlers in the game, players who are much taller, and stronger. Yet there is a drive and an energy that sets Michael Jordan apart from all the other players who ever played the game.

I'm not always high energy! Many with ADHD have a natural ebb and flow of energy. Sleep can be hard for those with ADHD. Because of our energy and sometimes our stress level, we may tend to shake body parts. I constantly move my feet all night while sleeping. Restless leg syndrome is very common in our world. I also believe that we tend to need less sleep than those without ADHD. There are days when three hours of sleep is all I need. If medicated, even less. As a leader, I had to self-talk myself out of sending emails or texts at 3:00 a.m. because I learned it makes others very nervous. Adjusting to your patterns instead of thinking they are just bad or wrong will make life much easier for you. I've found that when I take medication for my ADHD, I feel very tired when I come off it. I must remind myself when I feel sluggish that I'm not on my medication. I also find that I must plan those days out, so I don't have a big day when I have not taken my medication. That's a recipe for disaster!

One example that comes to my mind is referred to as the "flu game," which occurred in the NBA Playoffs between the Chicago Bulls and the Utah Jazz. Michael Jordan was so sick during this game that he had to be helped off the court during time-outs, then hydrated and iced down by the team's staff. At times during the game, he would be the only player not sweating and at other times he would be sweating profusely. Jordan won the game for the Bulls and had an incredible fourth quarter. This game was a testimony to his greatness, his desire to win, and to an extra reserve of energy and resilience to which those of us with ADHD can attest.

While not even close to the above example, I can remember playing in a lot of basketball games when I was very sick. I can remember on a couple of occasions where my mother took me to the doctor expecting the doctor to tell me that I should not play in the upcoming game. I am so thankful that my doctor refused to give my mother the satisfaction of hearing him say I could not play. The doctor told my mom that if I was too sick to play, I would not play and that if I became too sick, I would take myself out of the game. For whatever reason, I seemed to play very well when sick or in pain. The high-energy superpower is a gift to be treasured and should never be considered a deficit or a disorder!

High Energy in My Professional Life

Our high energy is seen by many as a detriment. As a kid, how often did you wish you could just *sit still*? It is not easy to manage our high energy. Those of us with ADHD must find work that is in our wheelhouse. I could never work at a desk all day. I cannot imagine being an accountant, banker, or grant writer. I worked on an assembly line for one summer while in college and hated it so much it actually motivated me to do better in school!

Both of my kids have ADHD and found jobs that perfectly match their ADHD superpowers. My son has his own technology company and my daughter is a nurse. Luckily for all of us, we found jobs where our excess energy and ADHD brains could thrive and be utilized. For all of us, the work is never finished. Each day is different and there is always more work to be accomplished than there is time.

My high energy allowed me to teach, coach two sports, raise my two children, write books, teach classes at a college, take courses to maintain my school administration license, and even play sports myself. I would argue that my high energy didn't just allow me to do all these but do them at a high level. As a school leader, coach, or athlete, I was often the first to arrive and the last to leave. I took on challenges that my peers would avoid like the plague.

And I would do so happily, even though it meant long hours and challenging debates. I truly think that many in my profession could not have done all I did without also possessing the high-energy ADHD superpower.

A Few Tips on High Energy

Below, I've listed some of my tendencies that I try to watch out for. These are aspects of my ADHD that I've realized can be problematic. I've also listed a few tricks I use to get around some of these high-energy challenges.

My Tendencies:

- I find it hard to sit through long lectures and boring meetings. I may have to get up and move around, which may come off as disrespectful. Unmedicated, I find it hard to listen all the way through a joke and then have to fake laughter, so the person thinks I listened and got the joke.
- I can have trouble falling asleep.
- I may go too fast on projects and leave out details or make silly mistakes.
- My continuous movement sometimes makes others nervous.
- Having high energy means those with ADHD are more likely to have accidents.

- Not everyone can keep up with me.
- I may try to do too much.

What I Do:

- Tell myself to slow down so I will not make as many mistakes. I will also ask myself if I am moving too fast.
- When needed, take medication.
- Always have other projects available to do in case I am in a situation where I could become bored.
- Find ways to use my energy for the benefit of the group. (Run to the store for last-minute shopping / be a runner for teachers if they need something from the office.)
- Play a sport and get plenty of exercise.
- Listen to music with headphones.
- Look for people I can help. Does the room need extra chairs? I will help carry them. Do we need to stack chairs after the event? Sign me up! As superintendent I would always put away chairs after large events with our custodians. I know the custodians and other staff enjoyed seeing the superintendent work. However, it was also helping me use my excess energy.

Superpower 3

Restlessness

"No one ever made a difference by being like everyone else"

—P.T. Barnum[7]

I believe mankind to be restless, which, in some way, propelled us to be at the top of the food chain. Our restlessness has enabled us to split the atom, cure disease, build massive cities, explore the depths of the ocean, travel to the moon—and now Mars—and has given us the ability to build atomic weapons that can ultimately destroy us. We seem to never be satisfied with the status quo.

For those of us with ADHD, the restlessness felt by human beings brews more intensely within our genetic makeup. There are the short-term restlessness issues like waiting in long lines, being stuck in traffic, being fidgety on airplanes, or having the inability to sleep thinking about the next day.

There are also the long-term restlessness issues like being bored with your job, home, marriage, or just life in general.

Football player Terry Bradshaw is considered one of the greatest quarterbacks in history. He led the Pittsburgh Steelers to eight AFC Central championships and four Super Bowl titles. Like so many other star athletes, Terry Bradshaw has ADHD. Besides being known as a Hall of Fame football player, Terry has many other interests and is a classic example of having the restlessness superpower that is so common among those of us with ADHD. Terry has been on several TV shows and has been the lead character in several movies. He is an author, songwriter, and singer. He's even been a horse enthusiast and breeder for over forty years. Bradshaw still works in football as an NFL analyst. It seems there's nothing he *won't* do, or at least try, and that is very common for those of us with ADHD.

However, the restlessness superpower also comes with challenges. Many of us know all too well the double-edged sword that is ADHD. Bradshaw admits to struggling with depression, having been through three divorces and other issues that are typical of those of us with ADHD. One such issue was being made fun of in school. He was often called stupid or slow. Early in his professional football career, the media mocked Terry's intellect. Before Super Bowl XIII, opponent Thomas Henderson said, "Terry Bradshaw couldn't spell cat if you spotted him the c and the a."[8]

Bradshaw responded, "This isn't nuclear physics, it's a game." Terry Bradshaw's Steelers won the Super Bowl and Terry was named the Most Valuable Player. Later, people joked that now Terry *could* spell MVP.

Michael Phelps, arguably the greatest swimmer in history, with twenty-eight Olympic medals, was diagnosed with ADHD at the age of nine. While he struggled in school, he found an outlet in swimming. He also has taken ADHD medication, stating, "I think the biggest thing for me, once I found that it was okay to talk to someone and seek help, I think that's something that has changed my life forever. Now I'm able to live life to its fullest."[9]

Restlessness has pervaded all aspects of my life. Professionally, I was a teacher for eight years while coaching two sports, then moved to another part of the state to become assistant principal and then principal. Next, I moved to another part of the state where I was promoted to associate superintendent and then one final move to superintendent. Besides teaching and coaching both at the school level and for my son's club team, I scored principal and superintendent exams for the educational testing in Trenton, New Jersey. I even had a paper route at that time! In addition to these jobs, I have also written five books over the last two decades. I have had three long-term relationships, have been married twice, and have lived in approximately fifteen different homes. You get the picture—I'm a rolling stone. You may be asking, how is this a superpower?

Career advancement was always a part of my life goals. However, as many can attest, changing jobs is stressful and most people only change when they must. Not so for me and my restlessness superpower. I've left great jobs simply because I wanted a change. In each instance, I sought advancement and, as you can see above, was able to achieve that goal. If it weren't for my restless spirit, I may just have stuck with my first job as a teacher and would have missed my true calling as a leader. I have my restlessness superpower to thank for my professional self-improvement and career advancement.

As a high school and college student I was always very shy, and I was really not a great communicator. After writing books, presenting, and leading at the highest level, I consider myself proficient at public speaking. My restlessness superpower is constantly forcing me out of my comfort zone.

When I retired from school administration, I started working for another company while I continued to write and present. I constantly stay busy over sixty hours a week to feed the restless feeling in my soul.

Being aware of this superpower, I know to look for jobs that give me freedom to be creative and allow me to perform different tasks within an organization. There are companies that pride themselves on their ability to be flexible with their employees' time and job skills. It also seems to be the way millennials are now choosing their places of employment. And in today's Covid-era workplace, people with ADHD have more options than sitting in a cubicle all day.

Find Your Happy Place

Many of us with ADHD need a place to escape to give our brains a rest. It could be taking a long shower or bath, or going to a bar or somewhere in nature. Several parents I spoke to have told me their kids take such long showers or baths they need to tell their kids to hurry up because the water bill is too expensive! The parents felt so bad when I mentioned it was probably because it was the only place their kid could just turn their brain off without distractions.

Similarly, the self-aware teacher with ADHD knows he or she cannot work in the same school at the same grade level teaching the same subject in the same classroom for thirty years. I know several people who have done this. Frankly, I admire that ability. However, it was painful for me to even *type* that scenario, let alone conceive that would be possible for me.

I know that I must seek new challenges to feed this superpower or life will not have meaning for me. New challenges for my job and my personal life are always needed. I used this knowledge to ensure that I wasn't moving on to another job in a new field starting over at entry level. I was able to prepare for my eventual need for a change of job to set myself up to advance my position. If you know that you have this superpower, embrace it, and enjoy the ride as you might have a chance to experience a level of excitement and joy those without ADHD cannot.

One final thought on my restlessness superpower. It has taught me to always be careful to avoid impulsive decisions that have long-term consequences. Here are a few tips:

1. Think (self-talk) before you quit your job. For example, you may need to be hired by someone else first. Remember, employers do not want to interview someone who has quit a lot of other jobs.
2. Do not buy your forever home early in your career.
3. Talk with your spouse or partner about your restlessness. By communicating this early, the partner knows to either buckle up or jump ship before they sign on for this wild ride.
4. Talk to your boss about your gifts. They might find ways to utilize you that feed your restlessness trait.

On the job, my restless spirit propelled me to take our school and school district customer service to a new level that I believe has never been matched. We would do small things like call all parents in the summer and have live people always answering our phones. We then trained all staff in customer service, while adding monitoring and rewarding mechanisms.

Eventually, we had every child receiving a home visit by a teacher in the summer before school even started. We won state and national awards for this program. We then created door hangers we could personalize when no one was home. The better we got at service the more career opportunities came my way. My thirst for customer service initiatives has never been quenched. I even keep tabs on the best customer service companies as they strive to constantly provide better service.

My restlessness has been a superpower that has allowed me to experience life to the fullest. Every day is like a party for me. While it is hard to find a lot of positive literature on restlessness, I would not trade my restless spirit for a calm life, with a boring nine-to-five job, even if it paid millions of dollars. Nor would I trade the opportunities to make friends at my various jobs throughout Kentucky and other states. Lastly, amid all my experiences I found the one perfect woman who gets me and my ADHD. Thanks, restlessness!

I asked my ADHD son, Russ, about his restlessness. He said he doesn't want to be normal. He doesn't want to be a cog in the wheel; he wants to reinvent it. That's a sentiment shared by many with ADHD. He finds desk jobs too unstimulating and wants to be involved in an industry that he thinks is making a difference in the world. How's that for a restless ADHD answer?

Tips on Restlessness

Our inherent restlessness can be detrimental to our well-being. We may get bored with our relationships, our jobs, our homes, or mundane parenting tasks. Sometimes it's just situations running their natural course, but some are instances of when we really need to stick to the decisions we've made. It can be hard to decipher one type from another, so we need some tools to help us work through these decisions.

- Self-talk as a reminder that I get bored very easily.
- Tell all my loved ones about my tendencies with this superpower.
- Listen to others before making decisions.
- Spend time reflecting on and analyzing big decisions— do not make major purchases or decisions without sleeping on them for a night or two.

- Look into the future and visualize the consequences of my decisions. For example, "After I make this decision, how long will it be before I am bored again?"
- Talk with others about similar experiences and what they may have done differently if given a do-over.
- Take ADHD medication and see if I still feel the same way about a decision.
- Find a friend I trust who will give me honest feedback about decisions. We need a critical friend who knows our ADHD tendencies.

Superpower 4

Hyperfocus

We all know one of the main "symptoms" of ADHD is the inability to pay attention. But those of us with ADHD know that's not quite accurate. There are times when we have ninja-like focus—when we can zero in on a single idea or activity and our attention *cannot* be broken. In cases like these, we've entered a state of hyperfocus, and it is a very important ADHD superpower.

In an article about adult ADHD for *New York Magazine*, Jenara Nerenberg says, "Writers, entrepreneurs, and creative leaders of all types know that intense focus that happens when you're 'in the zone.' You're feeling empowered, productive, and engaged. Psychologists might call this flow, the experience of zeroing in so closely on some activity that you lose yourself in it."[10] Does this sound familiar?

Hyperfocusing allows those of us with ADHD the ability to spend hours on a single task without a break. But it can be a tricky superpower to harness, as it requires just the right motivation to kick-start. Finding that motivation is a skill those of us with ADHD must learn if we are going to be successful in our personal and professional lives. For me, I've found a task, idea, job, or relationship needs to be fun, exciting, allow for movement, and be of interest to me. If not, it becomes obligatory, and I am only half-focused. Because of my leadership experience, when I am not focused I can still show fake interest in situations to a degree that most people cannot detect.

The ADHD superpowers mentioned in this book can work together and be activated simultaneously. Like how I used high energy and hyperfocus at the same time to accomplish my training goal for the 5K I ran with Amy. As you read, think about times when you've used multiple superpowers at once.

I've found in school we will work much harder for teachers we think care about us or in classes that fall within our ADHD wheelhouse. Classes like art, drama, technology, creative writing, and many others with teachers who care about us will get us extremely motivated. It is a combination of the right teacher in the right class that will make a difference in the world. One important factor is having a teacher who understands ADHD who can present information in a way that sparks our interest and gets us to work hard. For example, my high school literature teacher cared about me and turned me on to Shakespeare when we studied *Julius Caesar* and *Macbeth*. I can still quote the entire Mark Antony speech that begins "Friends, Romans, countrymen lend me your ears." To this day, forty years later, I love and attend Shakespearean plays. Thanks to the late Diane Ledford for inspiring me to love literature, and for truly caring about me.

Later in life, I was turned on to anything about leadership and would read everything I could on the subject. I became laser-focused on customer service and wrote several books on the subject. Then there was the time I got focused on children's literature that contained life lessons for adults. But it's not just reading that gets me into the hyperfocus zone. Currently, I am hyperfocused on pickleball to the point where I made a court at my house. At age sixty, I wonder where my next laser-focused endeavor will take me.

Hyperfocus in My Personal Life

Going into high school, I decided to try out for the tennis team. Having never played on a team before, I was the tenth best player out of ten members. I had fun learning the new sport, so starting out at the bottom did not bother me. However, in a short period of time, I learned that I had two advantages over most of my competition. Not only did I have an abundance of athletic ability, but I also had my ADHD superpowers of high energy and hyperfocus.

In fact, I would become hyperfocused on tennis every free moment. I would ride my bicycle to a park with tennis courts and look for people with whom to play. If no one was available, I would hit the ball off a backboard on the tennis court for hours. I constantly had blisters on my hand from playing so much tennis.

In those days, the top four players in the region went to the state tennis tournament at the end of the season. The only way to move ahead of players that were ranked higher was for the weaker player to challenge the player ahead of them. By the end of the season, I had moved from tenth to fifth and would be challenging a senior for the fourth spot to go play in the regional tournament. I remember the coach was very impressed with my movement up the ranks, but he did not think I would beat the senior for the fourth spot. Little did he know that only motivated me more to win. I ended up beating the senior and thus earned the right to play in the tournament. The coach pulled me aside and said he was going to let the senior play as this was his last chance to play in the tournament before graduating. I did not mind at all and the senior and I are even Facebook friends today. After all, everyone knew I had won the challenge. I had moved from the tenth best player to the fourth best player in the short two-month season.

Howie Mandel is famous for stand-up comedy and television shows like *Deal or No Deal* and *America's Got Talent*. While he famously lives with OCD, he has also talked about his experience with ADHD. "After I impulsively revealed that I have OCD on a talk show, I was devastated. I often do things without thinking. That's my ADHD talking," Mandel wrote. "Out in public, after I did the show, people came to me and said, 'Me, too.' They were the most comforting words I've ever heard. Whatever you're dealing with in life, know that you're not alone."[11]

My mother always said I had a gift for sports, and she always found a way to make sure I had the time to play. And I spent a lot of time practicing. I would get to practice early, stay late, and hit tennis balls off the backboard by myself for hours on weekends to get better. I had to be the best and I wanted to be the number one tennis player. This was my hyperfocus superpower manifesting. In my sophomore year I was the second best tennis player, moving past peers who had played their entire lives. I moved up to number one on the team in my junior and senior years and won the regional tournament at the number one position my senior year. I would go on to play tennis at Georgetown College for fun, as basketball paid the bills. My senior year, the tennis team went to the National NAIA Tennis Tournament for the first time in the history of the school. I have my hyperfocus superpower to thank for this commitment to being the best I could be.

Hyperfocus in My Professional Life

When I became principal at one of my schools, I found we needed to bring our test scores up. I hate being bad at anything—part of my competitive ADHD spirit—so seeing that my school was underperforming on state tests put a bee in my bonnet. Then my hyperfocus superpower kicked in. I read all the books about improving test scores and taught the teachers the best practices. I was on it all year. On the attendance report each day that went to all staff, I had a countdown to testing. The agenda would say 125 days until testing. My staff would later tell me I made them a nervous wreck about testing. I'm sure I was annoying to everyone, always talking about tests! Well, it turns out, after testing concluded, we went from one of the worst-performing middle schools in the state to one of the best in just one year.

Recently, coming home from a speaking engagement out of town, I got stuck in hours of traffic due to a car crash on the highway. I had discovered an educational video series I was into that I listened to on my way home. Well, when I got home at 4:00 a.m., I was more energized than when I'd left. I ended up staying awake until noon watching these videos, to the detriment of my sleep cycle. My hyperfocus had kicked in and nothing could get my mind off this topic. Many of us can relate. When something interests us, we dive deep and become an expert on the subject. So, while we may not be the best partner, friend, or coworker during these times, we can harness our hyperfocus superpower to meet our goals and keep us engaged with life.

Bending Time with the Hyperfocus Superpower

Hyperfocusing allows us to tune out noise and set our sights on a goal. This superpower can be even more effective when we use it to be more productive. That's where bending time comes in. People with ADHD can often become so hyperfocused that they become super-efficient and can work for long periods of time to accomplish a task that would usually take someone much longer to finish.

A great example of bending time is finals week in college. Everyone is cramming for their exams, trying to get so much studying in during a short period of time. Many of us with ADHD have the "symptom" of procrastination. However, I've found that during these cram sessions, I can get more done in a short period of time because it turns on my hyperfocus superpower and I can bend time.

My son, Russ, is a leader at a company that makes and runs high-tech kiosks across the country. Sometimes he spends months at a time at my home, where he has an office. Russ is very in tune with his bending time superpower. I have witnessed him go for days without sleeping and taking almost no time to even eat a meal. If I want to talk with him, I have to stand in front of his face and make him look at me. I get the reaction that would be very similar to waking someone up who is having a dream or bringing someone back after being hypnotized. Any communication with my ADHD son while he is hyperfocusing on a project goes unheard and unprocessed unless I stand right in front of him. As you would guess, I do my best to just stay out of his way during these times. The amount of work he can produce during these periods is incredible. Russ can do projects in two weeks that might take others several months. This is truly an example of bending time with ADHD.

One interesting theory I found about ADHD from *ADDitude* magazine offers an explanation of our hyperfocus. I talk about this theory in more detail later in the book. "The [Night] Watchman Theory posits that our hyperfocus and ability to give equal attention to every element in our environment is actually honed by evolution. The theory is that people with ADHD are wired to be the perfect night watchmen and hunters of our tribes and that most of our current advantages and disadvantages trace back to this vital role wherein our 'symptoms' would have saved lives."[12]

As a school leader, I once got a call on a Sunday afternoon that one of our buildings had been spray-painted by some kids the previous night. Those of you who have had to get business done on a Sunday know how hard it can be to mobilize people on this day. I needed to try to get this fixed before school resumed on Monday. I offered a reward to whoever found out who did it, contacted the people who could fix it, and communicated with the school board and principals. The spray paint seemed like it was everywhere—the side of the building, the buses, even the football fields—so we needed a miracle . . . or just good old-fashioned ADHD bending time! I didn't want the vandals to get the satisfaction of our kids and staff even seeing it on Monday. That *motivated* me to bend time, and my competitive nature kicked in to be sure we got this cleaned up before school started the next day.

I got the call while with my family at a Cincinnati Reds baseball game, so I had to take calls and was generally distracted by having to get this done. I eventually had to leave the game early. But the job got done and it was accomplished on time. Before the students could arrive at school the next day, we had every bit of graffiti removed from our campus. The vandals must have been so disappointed. The vandals had even hit other spots all across the city, which I saw for days and even weeks afterward. The city leaders did not have the same response time as this ADHD leader. I truly believe that using my superpower to bend time allowed us to do what all those other businesses and the city couldn't do within the same amount of time.

> Jim Carrey is known for his film roles in both comedy and drama. What many don't know is that he also has ADHD. One of the ways he uses his superpowers is by creating art. As a kid, being sent to his room was not a punishment, he says. It was a place where he could escape into his art, which, at the time, was drawing. In adulthood, he began painting and creating sculptures as an outlet for his creative energy.[13]

Another example of bending time was when a school within my district was preparing to put on a musical. I decided to drop in during the last week of rehearsals to see how it was going. The musical director was in her first year in the job and was having trouble with organization and time management. I realized she was in over her head, so I stepped in to help with some aspects that still needed work. Costumes and makeup didn't look good, the sound system wasn't working properly with the students' microphones, and the lighting wasn't synched up correctly, to name a few problems. I was able to get the whole crew and all administrators in the district to pitch in to make changes and improve it before opening night. It was a lot of work and there was some griping, but I think the musical was so much better because of our efforts. As a leader, sometimes the ability to bend time would make me unpopular because I expect others to have my level of dedication when there is an issue that needs to be fixed. I can cause a lot of stress on coworkers who might not work as well under pressure. Usually, though, the pressure pays off and they end up being glad I pushed them.

Setting a false deadline is one way I can game the system with my hyperfocus superpower. The false deadline works best the more immediate I can make it. If I say a task must be completed by tomorrow, I will not stop until the job is complete.

If I have a deadline thirty days from now and I do not use this hack, there is a good chance I will not start until the night before, regardless of the size of the job. This is also what happens to us in school as we will not start studying our material until the night before a quiz or test. We may be able to get by doing this early on in schooling, but as we progress through high school and college, it gets harder to do. Setting that false deadline stresses me out (in a good way!) and gets me in the zone early, so even if I don't finish that day, I've got time until the real deadline. Often, when I get into these deadline-driven zones, I find I'm able to be more efficient. I can cram in more tasks and get more done in a shorter period than normal.

Tips on Hyperfocus

- I might be so focused I ignore even my friends and loved ones, so I make sure to disconnect from my focused task before moving on to the next task. If I am still hyperfocused, I will not be in the moment when meeting people, attending functions, or listening to others. I've found that if I don't, people think I am antisocial, or I am mad at them.
- Tell others about this tendency and don't get mad at people who have the courage to disconnect me from this focus.
- Tell others when I need to go into this hyperfocus to perform this superpower. Tell them I am going to disconnect from anything and everything for a period of time. I make sure to remind them not to take it personally. In many cases, I may be going into hyperfocus to help those close to me, so they might need to be reminded of this fact.

Superpower 5

Creativity

"Life is too short to blend in"[14]

—Paris Hilton, model and
TV personality with ADHD

Creativity is a fun superpower for those of us with ADHD. It has been said that those with ADHD do not just think outside the box; we do not even know there is a box. We can use our unique way of seeing the world to put a fresh spin on something that others cannot even conceive. These are not just problem-solving instances, things that need fixing, but rather just being creative in our own way. It's what happens when we allow ourselves the freedom to ask, "Hey, what would happen if we tried doing this?"

Creativity in My Professional Life

Many years ago, as a new district administrator and parent, I went to enroll my daughter in her upcoming elementary school. When I called the school to ask who my child's teacher would be, the secretary said, "I will tell you but normally parents need to visit the front of our school and look through the glass window. The homeroom list will be posted two weeks before school starts and includes a list of needed school supplies." I told the secretary not to tell me any information as I wanted no favors . . . plus, I wanted to see what every parent had to go through each year. I drove up to the school and after a lot of searching, I found my child's teacher. I did not have a pen and paper to write down all the needed supplies, so I had to come back later to jot it all down.

This experience was eye-opening for me as a school leader. What about the 25 percent of children who live with their grandparents who may not be able to drive to the school? What about the parents who cannot afford this list of supplies? Why wait until two weeks before school starts? There just had to be a better way.

Daydreaming is an inevitability for many of us with ADHD. We'll often catch ourselves daydreaming and we don't even know it. This can be a problem when we are doing something important like driving or having a conversation. If you need to be present in a moment, perhaps self-talking to keep you on task can help. On the other hand, daydreaming can be beneficial to accomplishing tasks. Sports coaches often tell players to visualize scoring or making plays because of this benefit. So, if you find yourself daydreaming, try daydreaming about something you'd like to get better at!

My solution to this issue was to create Move-Up Day. On this day, students were allowed to meet their next year's teachers at the end of the current school year. Thus, students could envision their upcoming year, meet their future teacher, and see their classroom or perhaps school if they were moving up to the next school. The entire district was involved in this day, which we found alleviated a tremendous amount of anxiety for students and parents over the course of the summer. On this day, they also received a supply list and had all summer to shop. We also made some new requirements for supply lists as some of the requests were just downright crazy. This major district change helped ease the transition for our primary customer: the students. Another positive we did not anticipate was how much easier it made opening day of the next year. We even found that we did not lose as many students to other school districts because once students knew their next year's teacher, they did not want to change schools.

Initially, did anyone in the school district really like my creative solution? No way, but leadership is not about always playing it safe and keeping things the same. My ADHD creativity superpower saw this improvement and I ran with it. Not only did it prove an immediate success, but twenty years later both school districts I started these initiatives for still do a Move-Up Day.

Home Visits

The success of Move-Up Day led to home visits, which was a program I started to have every teacher visit each of their upcoming students' homes over summer vacation. The goal was to create a relationship between teacher and student even before the year began.

Once a teacher goes to a student's home and sees where they live, it puts the student's behavior into perspective and gives teachers more empathy for their students. We even saw our discipline instances go down after we started this program. Instead of sending students to the office for acting out, teachers began to speak with students after class and connect on a personal level to issues the student may have been having at home.

The MAGNA Award is a national award given to a few select districts in the nation for the most innovative school programs in the United States. This award is handed out at The National School Boards Association Conference each year. Both of my school districts where I initiated this program won the MAGNA Award. It was really validating to be surprised with an award for following my instincts and embracing my ADHD superpower.

Adam Levine is a judge on *The Voice* and singer of Maroon 5. He uses his creativity superpower to write his music, but it's not without its challenges. He says, "I had trouble sometimes writing songs and recording in the studio. I couldn't always focus and complete everything I had to. I remember being in the studio once and having 30 ideas in my head, but I couldn't document any of them." [15]

One final school example of using my ADHD creativity superpower was my decision to move discipline and nursing out of the main office. Some of you may remember being sent to the office when you acted out in class or kids being sent to the office because they had lice. I realized that it didn't make a great impression to have our disciplined and sick students in the same place new parents, students, and guests come for first impressions of our school. Moving these issues to another location in the school totally changed the atmosphere of our main office! I'm grateful that my school leaders and colleagues allowed me to utilize my creativity superpower to better our schools.

Creativity in My Personal Life

We all express creativity in various ways. Some of us write, paint, or do craft projects. I like interior decorating and enjoy making home improvements for my own home as well as others' homes. I cannot actually do much besides painting, but I like to come up with ideas and color schemes.

I also love landscaping, as it requires a certain type of creativity. When I need inspiration, I drive around looking at houses or search Pinterest. I decided I wanted some exterior lights all around my house, so I got quotes for professional installation. It turns out it was more than I wanted to spend, so Amy and I decided to do it ourselves. I provided the vision for the project, and she installed anything and everything I wanted. At night, our place now looks like a resort, and we saved thousands of dollars by doing it ourselves.

Other creative activities I enjoy include putting puzzles together, doing presentations, and writing books. Below I've listed a few jobs that some of my ADHD friends have turned into careers. My friends tell me their attraction to these positions was from a combination of freedom to express creativity and no two days being alike.

- Police officer
- Firefighter

- EMS
- Teacher and school administration
- Computer technician/security
- Landscaping
- Hairdresser/barber
- Actor
- Athlete
- Tour guide
- Musician
- Artist
- Entrepreneur

Amy knows that I have this creativity superpower, so generally, we separate duties in our marriage. While I am a creative thinker, only she is allowed to fix things and put things together. I am not handy when it comes to using tools or reading technical directions. In fact, I hate trying to follow directions so much I never would even try to put a model car together. My wife and I are so good about working within our strengths. Amy knows my superpowers and my limitations, and our only issues come when we do not stay in our lanes. One funny story about getting out of my lane is when Amy asked me to use a wrench because she could not reach the object she was trying to turn. I made one turn and the wrench slipped out of my hand and hit Amy right in the face. She cried, I felt terrible, and we eventually were able to laugh at how I was actually working in an area outside of my superpowers.

If you possess the creativity superpower, I suggest letting those around you know you have it. Let your boss know you are a creative thinker, and you would love to be involved in brainstorming sessions. Many with ADHD love meetings where ideas are considered without fear of being ridiculed. Our self-esteem improves when we know others liked or used one of our suggestions. Leaders with ADHD should be in brainstorming meetings and should get their employees with ADHD around a table and just ask for suggestions. When there is a problem, you need your creative ADHD people at the table.

Tips on Creativity

Here are some things I try to keep in mind when utilizing my creativity superpower.

- I may not have a job where creativity is valued. Is this job a good fit for me?
- I may have a boss who hates change. Not everyone appreciates creative new ideas.
- I may get upset when people do not listen or try my creative endeavors.
- My ideas may be so good that my boss takes credit for it. I need to be happy just giving myself credit.

- My creative thoughts may not work, or be dangerous. Some ideas are not worth the risk.
- I may spend so much time trying to be creative that I do not finish the task.
- Some creative ideas may just not be practical, and it may be hard for me to understand the big picture.
- Sometimes I will daydream about problems or ideas and will be taken out of the moment. This is particularly harmful when I should be listening to someone speak or when I'm driving.
- Do my best to get involved in decision-making. Tell my boss about this superpower.
- I should look for jobs where I can use my creativity superpower.

Superpower 6

Problem-Solving

"Too many rules get in the way of leadership. They just put you in a box. . . . People set rules to keep from making decisions."[16]

—Mike "Coach K" Krzyzewski

Our ADHD brains are wired a little differently. It's what allows us to think outside the box, be nonconformists, and express creativity. So, it stands to reason that we would also be good problem-solvers. I've found this to be true for most aspects of my life.

Problem-Solving in My Professional Life

Putting out fires is a huge motivator for me. I enjoy looking for problems and solving them. It allows me to use my superpower to think outside the box. Those of us with ADHD may want to avoid occupations where we do not have a chance to problem-solve, use our flexibility, and feel valued. Furthermore, we may not thrive working for leaders who never want to change or grow. In fact, my field of education really stifles change, progress, and thinking outside the box in favor of hiding behind laws and policy. I have been quite lucky to have worked with some open-minded teachers, leaders, and school board members who allowed me to use my problem-solving superpower to do what was best for our students. Considering how change-averse education is, my ideas could just as easily have led to me being fired. I like to say, given all the facts, a high school student could make 95 percent of all the decisions I made as superintendent. However, I get paid based on the other 5 percent. It's this 5 percent that makes all the difference, and problem-solving is at its core.

I have been involved in countless problem-solving endeavors as a school administrator. One such instance occurred during a year when our district had missed a lot of school because of snow and ice, causing the missed days to be tacked on to the end of the school calendar. To make matters worse, those extra days in June were exceptionally hot and humid. Our school district is in a very large county and some of our buses transported students over an hour away. The buses were miserably hot because back then our school buses did not have air-conditioning. Students would put their windows down but only hot, humid air circulated through the bus. Adding to the problem was our school's "no shorts" dress code. Of course, the media was right there interviewing students about the heat issues on the buses, adding to the tension of the situation. It didn't help that their presence and criticism proved to be justified when one of our students passed out from heat exhaustion. The students were suffering, and it was getting dangerous.

> "When something is important enough, you do it even if the odds are not in your favor." —Elon Musk

Our superintendent called me to a meeting of the top leaders including the transportation director, other central office leaders, and school principals. We brainstormed ideas to help our students with this issue, while also giving parents some comfort knowing we were at least trying to solve this problem.

About the best we could come up with was to allow students to wear shorts. While that was one of my suggestions, I seemed to be the only one in the room that was not completely satisfied. After all, I had children in the school system, and even though they did not ride the bus, as a parent, I would have been unimpressed with this meager school response. In this meeting, we had over one million dollars of salaries in the room, and I thought to myself, *Is this the best we can do?*

I spoke up and said I think as leaders we all need to ride a school bus with a long route so we can really see what it is like to be a student on one of our buses. I also said our ride should occur on a hot afternoon. After all, the best leaders walk in the shoes of their customers. No one liked that idea. I heard all kinds of excuses like, "We have plans, and where would we leave our cars? Some drivers take their buses home each day, so how could we make that work?" I quietly thought how much quicker *excuses* came from these leaders as opposed to *solutions*.

They ended up voting down my suggestion to ride the buses, but by now I had their attention on the issue. They knew when I got like this, the superintendent would always give me my say because I had several wins already in my pocket. By the time we left that day, we added some very creative solutions that we were able to carry out for several years in that district, including my eight years as superintendent.

1. Allowing students to wear shorts the last month of school.
2. Popsicles given to all students at the end of the day when temperatures reached ninety-four degrees.
3. Every student given a cold bottle of water before they got onto a school bus. Bus drivers and bus monitors also received water.
4. Communicating our plan to all parents, staff, and media outlets.

The next day we had media at schools taking pictures of all of us handing water to students as they boarded our thirty-three school buses. We had quickly flipped the negative press and opinion of our overheating school buses and were now receiving calls from other districts about our processes for making all of this happen.

As with any creative initiative, in the beginning there were doubters. Some bus drivers said the students would be throwing their bottles out the window, even going so far as to say they would not drive the bus if we gave students water bottles. Our superintendent held strong and said if they didn't like it, they could just turn in their keys and quit. Food service managers and directors complained as we had to use their freezers to get the water cold and house our popsicles.

We had each principal tell the students we were doing this for them and if there were any behavior problems with water bottles, we would quit offering this service. We never had one student disciplined for an issue with a water bottle, nor did any bus driver quit. They all now seem to look forward to these days. It was good public relations for our internal staff to witness our school leaders outside passing out water and interacting with our students, teachers, drivers, and aides.

The world found out that Simone Biles, the famous U.S. Olympic gymnast, had ADHD in 2016 from leaked Olympic medical records. While she may have been upset at the breach of her privacy, Biles took the opportunity to fight the stigma. "Having ADHD and taking medicine for it is nothing to be ashamed of nothing that I'm afraid to let people know," she wrote on her Twitter account.[17]

People with ADHD are creative problem-solvers who can think outside the box. Just like with our students, we need to tap into our staff members who have these superpowers and not dismiss their opinions and ideas before at least considering the possibilities.

This story also highlights how problem-solving differs from creativity because it requires a level of implementation that creativity may not. Decorating or painting can never truly be wrong, but when it comes to fixing a problem, it sure can go sideways without good problem-solving skills!

Problem-Solving in Sports

Being a college basketball player with limited natural talent as far as quickness and jumping ability, I always liked to watch former Boston Celtics star Larry Bird. Larry was tall but by NBA standards he was slow and could not jump very high. However, Larry is regarded as one of the best to ever play the sport. Regardless of the situation or how the defense played, he could figure out how to score points. In my own experience playing college basketball, I was expected to score at the guard position, which required me to have problem-solving skills on almost every play in every game.

When it comes to the problem-solving superpower, I always think about quarterbacks in football. They must read defenses and make changes on a moment's notice and communicate these changes to ten others within a limited time period. It is no coincidence that a much greater percentage of so many college and professional athletes have ADHD.

Problem-Solving in My Personal Life

I am attracted to problem-solving situations like setting up friends on dates. I never considered myself a matchmaker, but I find I can take people I know and find someone who would be a good fit for them. Maybe I've got a new career in the works! I believe I also found the love of my life and I want others to experience what Amy and I share.

Sometimes, it's those simple little things that our problem-solving superpower can fix to make life so much easier. While hanging a picture in my house, I wanted to hang it horizontally, but the fittings were set to only work vertically. I grabbed some wire, ran it from one fitting to the other, and presto! It could now be hung the other way.

As someone who experiences ADHD personally and as a parent, I know that sometimes we may pass down some of our idiosyncrasies. Often, without even knowing. I was sitting at dinner with my whole family one day and my son, who also has ADHD, mentioned he was at the gas station and drove away with the gas nozzle still in the car, ripping it right off. Everyone at the table dropped their forks and darn near choked on their food. Then there was me who just started laughing. They turned to me, and I said, "What? I've done that three times!" I now take time to look at the pump before ever getting in my car and pulling away. It may seem small, but this use of problem-solving may just save a few more innocent gas pumps.

Later in that dinner conversation, I learned my son and I both have walked into solid glass doors so hard that we were physically hurt. Those at the dinner who didn't have ADHD kept asking for more stories. I could see the aha moments when my kids and I described *why* we did some of these perplexing things over the years. Most of the time we were just hyperfocused on another task or just taking a brain break.

Business book author John Maxwell says always focus on your strengths. I knew grant writing was not my skill set. I would always delegate tasks like that so I wouldn't set myself up for failure. Delegating also allowed me to use my time on things that fit my skill set. I also hired detail-oriented people to balance out the needs of my schools and school districts as I led with my ADHD strengths.

It's true, those of us with ADHD are more prone to injury. However, getting hurt in innocuous everyday situations like walking around the house is more common than us getting hurt in dangerous situations. I like to say you want us around when danger is lurking as our adrenaline kicks in and our hyperfocus superpower takes over. We are the ones who spring into action to enter a burning building and help save people. That's problem-solving by simple action when others would run or just freeze.

Some of Fred Rogers's famous advice comes to mind here. Mr. Rogers said when he was younger and he would see scary things in the news his mother would say, "Always look for the helpers."[18] I say when you have an emergency, look for the people with ADHD. Stress and adrenaline will give our brains dopamine, which will then activate our superpowers. We will be calm and laser-focused as we use our problem-solving skills to help save the day. Those of us with ADHD wear an invisible logo under our shirts that states, "Call on me when you have an emergency." We are the "helpers" of whom Fred Rogers was speaking.

Divergent Thinking

As a symptom of ADHD, divergent thinking can be described as not being able to see things the same way as others. In some circumstances, it can be hard for those of us with ADHD to relate to how others interpret a situation. For problems that require a specific method or answer, we may be off base. Like showing your math when you know the answer but don't go about it the way the teacher asks. Or when discussing a novel in English class, where there are the more obvious connections one can draw, which most of the class picks up on, yet the ADHD student sees a vastly different meaning behind the same symbolism. In these situations, teachers may think we are "not getting it," when we are just seeing things differently. Our grades may suffer, and we may not be able to get our point across, which can result in us becoming frustrated.

However, our divergent thinking can also help fuel problem-solving in many situations, as it allows us to come up with solutions many who think convergently cannot. We may not be good at thinking of consensus ideas, like answering questions on *Family Feud*, but we can be great at problem-solving and thus be incredible on *Survivor*.

Tips on Problem-Solving

When your boss says they want honest feedback in front of a group of people, many times they really do not. For those people who do not know our superpowers, we may make some people angry by giving suggestions or opinions at the wrong time. We want to make the world a better place and think we need to give opinions and solutions right now. I now try to read situations and people, understand timing, slow down, and ask myself if there is possibly a better time to make this suggestion. For example, when my wife comes home from work and tells me all her problems, she generally just wants me to listen.

We also tend to interrupt people with our thoughts because we do not want to forget them. We must self-talk, understand timing, and make sure this is the right time to give advice.

- Self-talk—does the person really want suggestions?
- Is this the appropriate time to give the suggestion?
- Do not get offended if no one likes my suggestion.
- Look for ways to help people.
- Be ready to oversell my idea because it may seem out of left field to others.
- Try to get into a room where decisions are made.
- Let those around me know about my superpower so I can be of use to them.

Superpower 7

Quick Starter

Have you ever brought home a device or piece of equipment and took one quick look at the instructions and then just started using it? Many of us with ADHD hate instructions. We just want to get to it. It can be perceived as impulsiveness, impatience, or simply not following directions—the "symptoms" of ADHD—but I think it's just that we are quick starters. I find this superpower especially useful when having to make group decisions. "Analysis paralysis" is a real problem with committees, and while it's dangerous to jump headfirst into the water without knowing how deep it is, we don't need a sonar scan of the bottom of the lake before we know it's safe to dive into. The ADHD quick starters can be the signal to stop deliberating and act. Or, as businessman and politician Ross Perot said, "If you see a snake just kill it—don't appoint a committee on snakes."[19]

If you look in my kitchen cabinets at home, you'll notice half the cereal boxes are upside down. It seems I can't even be bothered to look at the box to see which is the top before I open it. I have exploded so many bags of chips because I do not take the time to read how to open them. Other times, after I finish with my snack, I am not able to seal the chips back up correctly, so they are stale the next time I go to eat them. That's the quick starter trait in a nutshell.

Quick Starters in Business

I love the saying "Sometimes you need to build the plane while you are flying it." In other words, it's not always feasible to think something through fully before implementing it. Elon Musk, the notorious quick starter and tech billionaire, made news in 2023 when his SpaceX starship test flight exploded after four minutes in the air. His response on Twitter was, "With a test like this, success comes from what we learn."[20] That's one of the advantages of being a quick starter. In 2022, the entrepreneur and risk-taker made the controversial move to buy the social media platform Twitter, now known as X. The changes he made, like changing the user verification system, making huge personnel cuts, and loosening oversight of dangerous and misleading posts, left people scratching their heads. It seems he didn't care to sit around in meetings or run focus groups to ensure these were sound ideas—he just implemented them. In a 60 *Minutes Overtime* interview, he said, "If something is important enough, you do it even if the odds are not in your favor."[21] That's the quick starter mentality to a T.

I've found those of us with ADHD tend to have an entrepreneurial spirit. We tend to become frustrated or agitated with minutiae and details, but coming up with new ideas or starting a big initiative is truly in our wheelhouse. An article in ADDitude magazine discusses the presence of people with ADHD in the entrepreneurial world. "ADHD entrepreneurs think fast, talk fast, and move fast. They act first and think later. 'Those with ADHD tend to spur themselves into action regardless of uncertainty,' says Johan Wiklund, Ph.D., a professor at Syracuse University who studies entrepreneurship. 'An impulsive inability to wait comes with a willingness to take risks. The [ADHD entrepreneurs] I studied struggle. But if they had a chance to be like everyone else, none of them would take it.'"[22]

Another quote from that article, by ADHD coach Tracy Otsuka, elaborates, "We have to be in action, or we are not happy. To be 'driven' is a form of hyperactivity. That is the entrepreneurial trait in a nutshell."[23]

These quotes just reinforce that it is in our nature to jump right into projects, and even if we don't get it right the first time, we'll figure it out eventually. That's the quick starter superpower.

Quick Starter in My Professional Life

I always want people to just get to the point when they're talking to me. People tend to talk with a lot of fluff in their speech. It's just how most people communicate. As someone with ADHD, I have to self-talk to keep from interrupting and saying, "Get to the point!" As a school administrator, I always told people to cut out the pleasantries. I know the reason they're calling or coming into my office is because of a problem, so just come out with it. I came to be known as a no BS leader, which helped my image, but it's just naturally part of my ADHD quick starter superpower.

In my professional life, my ADHD superpowers are not going to allow me to waste time in meetings by being slowed down by bureaucratic practices. As I mentioned earlier, in public education, it is not politically advantageous for leaders to make lots of changes. I would get my best people together, discuss an initiative, and we would generally start quickly. Sure, we'd go over all the steps and take time to sell initiatives, but we did not spend a lot of time in baseless, boring meetings. If something was best for kids, we did not need a lot of time to keep talking things through.

Take the implementation of our home visit program, for example. I felt very strongly that we needed this change in our school system because it would build relationships between students and teachers. However, I knew there was a group of employees who would oppose this program because their job is to stop change whenever possible. Keep in mind, these are the people who will panic if you move a copier to the other side of the faculty lounge. I made sure I thought out solutions to their biggest objections so those anti-change agents couldn't gain any momentum to block it. Because of that, we were able to quickly push the initiative through. Within a few years, our home visit program won two prestigious national awards and numerous state awards. Later in my career, I implemented a home visit program in another district with the same results. Had I not followed my quick starter superpower, meetings and committees would have taken over and the anti-change people would have slowed down or killed the initiative.

When I decided to pay for teachers' lunches any time they sat to eat and talk with our students in the cafeteria, I did not spend a lot of time putting together a committee to decide on the feasibility of this program. When I heard another district was allowing students to decide which teacher would hand them their diploma, I did not ask for a lot of other opinions. It was a wonderful idea, so I implemented it. The school board hated giving up this responsibility at graduation and told me so. After the first graduation, seeing students and their favorite teacher hugging and crying onstage, no one ever questioned this decision again.

Quick Starter in My Personal Life

I never take a lot of time to make decisions. I seem to have this ability to look at an issue and get right to the heart of the matter. I have moved several times in my life, and each time I'm considering a new place, I ask myself, *Will I like my home more, is the location better, can I afford it, and is my wife on board?* I can make this decision in thirty minutes. That just might be why I have moved fifteen times since graduating from college!

I am just not going to spend mental energy on buying a car, a suit, or other items many mull over. I am also not going to spend a lot of time planning a vacation because I know I'll have fun anywhere I go. I also don't want to be booked solid so I can have spontaneous adventures.

This superpower has allowed me to have more free time in other areas of my life, be more spontaneous, and take advantage of opportunities when they arise. I am going to be a quick starter in anything I do, and you will not catch me wasting a lot of productive time in boring meetings, unnecessary planning sessions, or mundane tasks in either my private or personal life.

Actress and musician Zooey Deschanel, who you may know from the TV show *New Girl* or one of her many movies, has said she does not take medication for her ADHD. Instead, she prefers to take on hobbies that keep her creative mind busy without needing to commit to long projects. Her activity of choice is crafting, and she has shared some fifteen-minute craft ideas on HelloGiggles.[24]

My son tried playing pickleball with me one time. He'd never played, and I started going over the rules, but he said, "Nope, Dad, let's just get started." I said, "You don't even know how to play yet." He insisted, he'd learn as we go. He couldn't be bothered to wait thirty seconds for me to explain the handful of rules. Hell, he *enjoyed* learning on the fly like that. I recognized his ADHD trait, and we just started the game. Had I taken time to go over all the rules, he may have just quit, and I would have missed out on a great father/son moment. I couldn't blame him either. I can't stand when I sit down to play a board game with people, and someone insists on busting out the manual and reading every single rule. Of course, there are plenty of times those of us with ADHD find out we've been playing a game wrong for many years!

Tips on Quick Starter

- I may move too quickly for those on my team or in my family. I must take the necessary time to build trust and sell my ideas to the people closest to me in my personal and professional life.
- I may not have taken the time to research a decision and thus have missed out on other opportunities or important details. I surround myself with detail-oriented people who can read the fine print for me.
- When pitching an idea to others, know my tendencies and self-talk about the change process and then take the time to sell all the necessary information. Tell myself that "people support what they help create."
- Self-talk when dealing with detail-orientated people knowing that I need these people in my work life and personal life.
- I have also made mistakes in haste, could have possibly found better deals, or could have had more patience for situations.
- Get plenty of rest. I have noticed I am a lot more impatient when I am tired.
- Take my medication when needed. There are times when I really need to take my medicine to activate my ADHD superpowers, just like Popeye with his can of spinach.
- Self-talk about including everyone in the decision-making process. Knowing that trust takes time is one of the most important components of leadership.

Superpower 8

Risk-Taking

"I'd rather regret the risk that didn't work out than the chances I didn't take at all."[25]

—Simone Biles, Olympic gymnast with ADHD

I n Chapter 4, I referenced the "Night Watchman" theory of ADHD. Many researchers[26, 27, 28] have noticed the superpowers of the ADHD brain line up with many of the survival skills necessary in the earlier days of humans. It could have been that those with ADHD, who are more prone to risk-taking, volunteered to spy on enemy camps or stay up all night to protect their own camp from saber-toothed cats or other predators. That extra energy could have also been useful for hunting and the risk-taking superpower would have made large prey less intimidating to their ADHD brains. All these factors would have made those with ADHD especially important during the hunter-gatherer times in human history. But how is this a superpower today?

I mentioned earlier the teacher who taught the same subject in the same classroom from their first year of teaching to their retirement over thirty years later. For someone like me, that would be an amazing accomplishment, but there is just no way I could have been an effective teacher for very long under those circumstances. I need new challenges and new risks in order to thrive. It's what allowed me to go up the ranks from teacher to superintendent, taking the chance at the next level each time and even moving my family to new places. Those were very risky moves, considering education's tenure laws. In my state, after four years, a teacher is tenured and basically cannot be fired. However, when you leave your district and move to another district, you lose your tenure rights for one year. Three times I took a leap of faith and changed schools, changed districts, changed jobs, sold homes, and eventually divorced and went through several relationships. Risk-taking is dopamine to the ADHD brain and thus we thrive in such environments. I mentioned earlier that those with ADHD may gravitate toward entrepreneurship. We may be more likely to take risks because we just cannot stand being bored on the job.

Michelle Rodriguez, the actress who starred in *Lost* and the Fast and Furious movie franchise, has spoken about a dilemma many of us with ADHD grapple with: take medication or don't? She says, "I want to write and direct, but it's not easy with ADD. I have a hard time focusing when I'm alone. I'm a scatterbrain, but I'm nervous taking medication. I don't really want to depend on anything to control my brain."[29]

Looking back on my life, I consider the many great friendships and the personal growth that occurred in me through these years and believe risk-taking is a superpower that has allowed me to take a chance and push my abilities. If I had been risk-averse, I'd still be the same teacher in the same district where I started. There's nothing wrong with that, but I am very happy my ADHD pushed me into school and district leadership roles, and I am thankful to have had the opportunity to work in several schools and districts in various teaching and leadership roles.

Risk-Taking in My Personal Life

I have so many examples of when risk-taking paid off in my life it was hard to choose just a few for this book. I truly think the risk-taking superpower allows those of us with ADHD to become successful both personally and professionally. One such risk was truly life-changing for me. At age fifty-three, I decided to take a risk and put myself out there on a dating app. As superintendent, this made me nervous on many different levels. What would my school board think when they inevitably found out? Would I be laughed at in the community? Would I lose the respect of my peers? My ADHD superpower gave me the ability to take a chance. Within a week I met my soulmate, Amy. I cannot imagine my life without her, and I am eternally grateful that my risk-taking superpower won out over my fears and self-doubt.

> "When I am 80, I don't want people to say, 'What a nice old man.' I want them to say, 'OMG! What the hell is he up to now?'"[30]

There are other areas where this superpower comes into play as well. Risk-taking has resulted in a very fun-filled, exciting life for me and I cannot imagine living any other way. I love blowing things up with M-80s on the Fourth of July (more on this later), working in the top of tobacco barns to make extra money, and painting from the tops of very high ladders, to name a few. After turning fifty-five, I began to rent fast cars in Las Vegas that went two hundred miles an hour. I also learned to shoot guns and even tried various forms of THC. At age fifty-eight, I climbed to the top of Mokoli'i in Hawaii. For those not familiar, search for an image of this steep, rocky island. It started raining after I made it to the top and I was very blessed to make it to safety without serious injury or death. Because of this superpower, I truly live life to the fullest and will not have any regrets when I leave this earth. Is it any wonder that people just seem to want to be around me? Is it any surprise that I generally get invited to events? People just know that I am going to bring the fun.

Tips on Risk-Taking

We have more accidents than others and thus we tend to live fewer years than our non-ADHD peers. Depending on the research, it can be between ten and twenty years less.[31] So, before you stretch too far while on that ladder, ask yourself if a fall is worth the extra two inches of paint in that corner. Might I become paralyzed or die if I fall from this height? Take your time, get down, and move the ladder over another foot. Many times, the risk is just not worth it.

- Risk-taking in my professional life could have caused me to be unemployed or even financially ruined. Especially if I had worked for the wrong type of leader. I always self-talk when making big professional decisions and ask the opinions of others to avoid making a snap decision. I would also recommend sleeping on big decisions as almost every decision can wait at least one night.
- Risk-taking can cause serious injuries in your personal life. I try to look into the future and at least do a worst-case scenario analysis before I attempt to take a risk. I ask myself, *Is the risk worth it?*

- A word of warning: those of us with multiple ADHD tendencies like risk-taking, quick starting, or creativity can multiply our chances of accidents leading to serious injuries. It is important to be aware of these tendencies. When you think of the sheer number of people with ADHD older than fifty who have never been diagnosed or medicated combined with the ADHD folks who do not know how to self-talk or harness their ADHD superpowers, it is no wonder that our life expectancy is much lower than those without ADHD. For the same reason, combining our tendencies without training, self-talk, and other hacks can also lead to broken relationships, job loss, and other hardships.

Superpower 9

Multitasking

Many of us with ADHD will thrive in chaos and are not as overwhelmed by lots of stimuli. Have you ever heard someone say they feel like they are overloaded? Well, welcome to our everyday world as I have felt this way my whole life. Since overload is normal to me, everything else generally leads to boredom. Many of us with ADHD enjoy having lots of stimuli—hence the multitasking superpower.

Some may think that multitasking is not a superpower. To that I would say to watch someone with ADHD juggle several activities at a time. For me, I know how to give myself several tasks at the same time and rotate between tasks quickly.

Multitasking in My Professional Life

As a principal, I loved working with middle school students. Their energy, short attention spans, and overall loudness were stimulating to me. I know a lot of people in education for whom working in a middle school classroom would be their worst nightmare. But being a teacher and school administrator at this level were perfect jobs for this guy with ADHD.

In my role as school leader, I was constantly inundated with new problems. When faced with a handful of tasks to accomplish, I would get in the zone and look forward to the challenge. It's much like the feeling that coffee or caffeine gives people. I would run from task to task and most of the time would not fully complete any of them—completion of a task would be cutting down on the chaos that I seem to enjoy. However, constantly finding more tasks will motivate me to want to complete the original task, thus creating a cycle of inspired energy. Self-talk is also an essential part of coming back to those original tasks and not forgetting about them.

Actor, producer, and rapper Will Smith has been a staple in entertainment for decades. Those familiar with his energy can see why he is one of the many born before the 1990s who consider themselves undiagnosed ADHD. In 1998 he shared with *Time* magazine: "I was the fun one who had trouble paying attention. Today they'd diagnose me as a child with ADHD."[32]

Multitasking in My Personal Life

Now, most research says that multitasking with work can be less productive.[33] Human brains can't truly concentrate on two things at once . . . or can they? I believe there are times when I am actually better because I'm doing multiple projects at one time. I also believe there are ways to game the system with this superpower. Research has found that using senses other than the primary one can increase focus and attention for those with ADHD.[34] For example, listening to music while doing homework, doodling while listening to a lecture, chewing gum while taking a test, or moving in any way while concentrating on a task can help us with concentration. Fans of the TV show *The West Wing* may recall the famously long "walk and talk" scenes—a great strategy to get the ADHD brain in high gear! I used this strategy often when I was a principal and superintendent, walking and talking with my staff through the school on our way to our destinations and at the same time increasing our visibility to the students.

When I'm considering taking on multiple projects, the first thing I do is choose my simultaneous tasks wisely. For example, I would not choose to vacuum while on a Zoom call. However, I like to cook. So cooking a large dinner using multiple burners, microwaves, and ovens puts me in my element and allows me to unleash my multitasking superpower. Not only am I preparing several dishes at once, but I am also making sure they are all complete at basically the same time!

When humans were hunter-gatherers, those with ADHD were rock stars. We had the energy to work, travel, and hunt. We were the ones who would hunt and kill the saber-toothed cats that got too close to our camp. However, in today's school world where we have to sit and be quiet for eight hours, we are now diagnosed with a disorder!

I may also choose to do some writing while cleaning. So, when I'm vacuuming the house, I'll do one room, stop and do some writing, then go back to vacuuming. As a bonus, I can brainstorm while vacuuming. I find this physical activity stimulates my creativity. I can also reflect or brainstorm while mowing the yard or walking. Many of my big school and district decisions were made while I was mowing the grass.

I think there are situations when doing multiple tasks makes me perform *better*. The reason is that switching tasks gets my adrenaline going and activates my high energy and hyperfocus superpowers, which allow me to be more efficient with my time on task. The trick is knowing how long I can spend on one task before my adrenaline wanes and I start to spin my wheels or lose that productivity edge. Having that second task queued up to switch over to, reengaging my high-energy/hyperfocus superpowers, allows me to keep that adrenaline flowing and that efficiency at a maximum. For example, when working with others in a meeting, I may be listening, but I can often let my mind work on my own ideas and come up with a new angle. If I had been sitting in my office concentrating on coming up with a new idea, I probably wouldn't have had it, but having this other stimulus—someone else talking—boosts my creativity and problem-solving superpowers. Now, there is a trade-off. I may miss a detail from the person speaking, so I must weigh the cost of trying to listen and letting my ADHD brain do its thing. Often, the outcome of solving a big problem at the expense of a few minutes of hearing another person is a good trade-off. But I do have to be sure to multitask in a judicious manner, always respecting those who are in front of me speaking.

There are bound to be differences in abilities in preferences between the ADHD mind and the non-ADHD mind. Some people would hate to spend ten minutes on one thing and then switch to another, but for me, that's perfect! My editor, Mike, had a creative writing class in high school where the teacher would have them write for a few minutes, then read a poem, then talk about it, etc., bouncing from one activity to another the whole time. He said it was so frustrating just getting into the groove and having to switch gears like a car constantly upshifting and downshifting. If it were me, I would have loved that class structure each and every day.

This same phenomenon happens when I'm writing my books—I often come up with my best ideas when on a call listening to my editor when I'm struggling to come up with content on my own. I love walking, talking, and thinking when working on my books. It is my most creative time.

In other situations, I find I can better concentrate when there's something else going on. For example, watching a movie and doing something on my phone. Let's face it, TV can be predictable and sometimes my ADHD brain is two steps ahead of the plot. In those times, I can answer emails, have a conversation with a friend, or play a game on my phone. I'm able to follow the TV and also perform other tasks—in both instances just as well as or even better than if I'd only been doing just one. There is some evidence to support this idea as well, using the term *continuous partial attention*.[35]

My Funny Trip to the Doctor

For those who do not take ADHD medication, you may not know that in order to refill Adderall (at least in my state) a visit to the doctor's office is required. Patients need to have routine checkups, which include a urine sample. My visits to refill my prescription are usually no big deal, but on one occasion I had made an all too common ADHD error. Being a school superintendent at the time, I had a few other things on my mind as I got checked in and the nurse handed me the urine collection bottle. As I entered the restroom, I placed the bottle on the shelf and then proceeded to urinate in the toilet. After finishing, I washed my hands and then noticed I forgot to urinate in the bottle. It is quite embarrassing to walk out of the restroom and tell the nurse you forgot your only task. While she laughed and probably thought that was why I needed medication, I cannot help but wonder if she questioned me being in charge of an entire school district! I went to McDonald's and got a cup of coffee and then went back to the doctor's office to try again. As I stated previously, we all make silly mistakes, but for those of us with ADHD, our mistakes happen a little more frequently.

Multitasking can be a good thing for our ADHD brains. However, we must be very self-aware of our ADHD superpower. There are times when situations may call upon our multitasking superpower and there are other times when we do not need to open up this can of spinach. Hopefully, the resources and examples in this chapter will help you decide on when and how you use this superpower.

Tips on Multitasking

- I've learned the conditions where multitasking is a bad idea for me. If I'm tired or if I am taking on two tough tasks at once, it is usually a bad idea. Then there are certain jobs where I want to avoid multitasking. For example, balancing my checkbook and memorizing a presentation for work is too much brain power all at once. Physical work, on the other hand, like baling hay, painting, or working on projects for home renovation, is easy to multitask for me and thus activates my superpowers.

- My tendency to multitask can also be a detriment at times. I find myself working on all different projects at once and making mistakes that I need to go back to later and fix, which ends up taking more time than if I'd just done one of them at a time. When those things happen, it not only costs me time and money, but also causes frustration and, honestly, makes me feel stupid.

- I have a tendency to be in multitask autopilot. But there are times and situations when this is not necessary. For example, when someone is speaking, I need to just focus on the speaker and what they are saying. Allowing my mind to go astray while someone is talking will keep me from hearing important information, including the person's name. A big one for me!

- I might get frustrated, make several mistakes, or just quit a project. I try to stay calm and keep this superpower under constraints. I've found I get especially frustrated when new tasks get added when I'm in the middle of my other tasks. Adding one or two new tasks when I'm already working on ten is a big deal for me. My wife has learned not to pile on when I am already in multitasking mode.
- I stay aware of situations and surroundings. If I'm at a party and everyone is talking, I should also not be on my phone texting with others or watching TikTok videos.
- One of the most dangerous situations is when I start daydreaming when I'm driving. When a road ends or lanes merge and I don't concentrate on driving in those situations, I find myself having close calls. Sometimes I even find myself checking texts while driving. Self-talk saves my bacon usually, but it's still a struggle for me.

Superpower 10

Spontaneity

I n our daily lives, being spontaneous can be beneficial. On a regular day, if you and your partner plan to go to dinner, that could be a nice evening. But, if five o'clock rolls around and you say, "Hey, let's go out to dinner," it changes the expectation from a boring old evening at home to a fun, impromptu evening out. Now, even though the activity is the same, sometimes the surprise of a spontaneous dinner out can be more enjoyable than a planned one.

This is a great superpower to use because it not only allows me to be "impulsive" but also brings joy to others, which, as I'll talk about in another chapter, is also an ADHD superpower. Life is short and we know the final outcome. Enjoying this life is a top priority for me and therefore I consider spontaneity a very special superpower.

Spontaneity in My Personal Life

Over the years, I've learned how to use my impulsivity as a superpower. Being *spontaneous* can help you connect with people through their fun side. I have realized that experiences that just naturally occur seem to be more enjoyable to me than planned events. I believe that applies to a lot of people and not just the ADHD brain. When we are on vacation, we have a lot of fun when we do something spontaneous. I will access my "impulsiveness" to make the moment more fun for myself and those around me. In fact, I schedule in time for spontaneity when I go on trips. Amy, who is always very well-planned, realizes our trips are much more fun when she allows me to just go with certain moments. She has even learned not to have rigid schedules on any of our trips. Recently, we were on a trip to Boston walking around the city. We were at a bar and were offered tickets to see the Celtics play an NBA playoff game. At first, Amy was not interested. She's not a fan of basketball and the tickets were expensive. My spontaneity superpower kicked in and she reluctantly agreed. Sure enough, the atmosphere in the Garden was so electric within the first few minutes of the game she was cheering right along with the Celtics crowd as if they had been her favorite team since birth. Amy even purchased a shirt to show her team support. We ended up having a blast, possibly the highlight of our trip, and we'd had no intentions of even going just a few hours earlier.

This superpower is of great use at any party. Many of you may know, we can be the life of the party because we can live in the moment in ways many people cannot imagine. If Amy and I are at an event and we are not having much fun, she will find ways for me to open up that can of spinach and unleash this superpower. She will poke and prod me until I do. There are times we have been at functions after I have been medicated and I have overheard Amy tell people that I will not be as much fun tonight because I took medication. Medication seems to make me quieter in social settings and requires me to work extra hard to access my spontaneity superpower.

> Terry Bradshaw, four-time Super Bowl champion, has embraced his ADHD over the course of his lifetime. But it wasn't always easy. Some of us may recall a story like Terry's as he says, "I don't think it was any different for a lot of the folks back in the '50s, early '60s. Children like me spent most of their time in a corner or up by the teacher's desk. We're the ones who wouldn't shut up or be still and who didn't particularly do very well in class. We didn't realize we had ADD or any other mental illness. We just, you know, couldn't sit still."[36]

Amy has a great awareness of my strengths and ADHD tendencies. However, in a moment of frustration, it's easy to forget. We all need to be reminded from time to time about our superpowers and our tendencies. Those of us with ADHD also cannot use it as an excuse for rudeness or bad decision-making. On one particular day, a reminder and also an apology was needed.

Amy had been working very hard on our landscaping and it was getting dark outside. She just needed a little more light on the side of the house to finish. As I was going into the house to clean up, she asked me to turn on the side light where she was finishing the job. I said sure, walked into the house, and then some news story caught my attention. Can you guess what happened next? I forgot about the lights and Amy outside working. About thirty minutes went by when Amy threw open the door and she let me have it for not turning the light on. I said as soon I came into the house this breaking news story was on TV and caught my attention. I knew I needed to stay on task, but I impulsively watched the TV and quickly forgot about my mission.

Knowing in this situation I needed more ammo I said, "You know what you married before you said, 'I do,' and you do not like for me to take my Adderall." She looked at me and we both just started laughing. I apologized with empathy and that was that. This brief reminder helped Amy to know that my actions were not intentional, and I was not being disrespectful . . . at least not on purpose. I apologized because I still cannot use my tendencies as an excuse. Since an apology wasn't really enough, I also helped her complete the project. In retrospect, I could have begun my self-talk as soon as Amy requested for me to turn on the lights. Self-talk would have kept me repeating Amy's request in my head until the lights were turned on. Impulsivity got the best of me, but it was a good chance to remind Amy about my tendencies. We joked about it later that night and enjoyed telling our family members about one of our first big arguments.

Spontaneity in My Professional Life

A company I am consulting for was having an off-site retreat at their headquarters in Pittsburgh. The president was there, and we were discussing our work and then went to a planned dinner. We had some free time afterward that was unstructured. Cue the spontaneity superpower. I persuaded everyone to go bull riding and then to a casino for gambling. Some of the people had never played casino games and we had fun teaching everyone the rules. Even though we had to get up early the next day to work, we stayed at the casino until 3:00 a.m. Doing something spontaneous allowed us to have more fun than anything we could have ever planned.

Strong leaders with ADHD need to remind everyone of their tendencies. I can remember times when my inner circle of leaders around me would get frustrated because I would take a project almost to completion and then just walk out and leave. Yes, I should have been self-talking, but we are not perfect. My inner circle leaders would ask in a very strong way for me to stay and finish the project. The key is that I would never get mad at them, and I would even thank them later for that reminder. They would also shorten meetings for me because they knew the limits of my attention span. Sometimes, I would tell them, "Do not worry today. I am fully medicated!"

> This quote covers my dining room wall: "Life should not be a journey to the grave with the intention of arriving safely in a pretty and well-preserved body, but rather to skid in broadside in a cloud of smoke, thoroughly used up, totally worn out, and loudly proclaiming 'Wow! What a Ride!'" —Hunter S. Thompson[37]

My awesome administrative assistant Kim would work 24-7 if a task needed to be completed before the next day. However, when I asked her to send a blistering email to someone, she would take her time and wait until the next day. I would then ask her if she sent the email the next morning and Kim would tell me this little white lie that she got so busy she could not get to it until the next day. She then would ask if I still wanted to send it. Many times, we did not send these emails or letters, and other times I decided to tone down the language. Kim was giving me a night to sleep on it before the email or letter went out. When you are honest about your superpowers and tendencies, the people around you are more likely to support you. I always knew she was playing this game for my benefit. My last month before retirement I told her I knew she had been doing this little trick in my best interests for eight years and thanked her for taking such great care of me. She said she knew I knew about this game. Those of us with ADHD who lead others need someone like Kim in our lives.

Moments of Regret from Impulsiveness

As previously stated, studies show that people with ADHD typically do not live as long as those without ADHD. Accidents are one of the leading causes of death for those with ADHD and it's often our impulsiveness that is to blame.

I need to constantly remind myself not to be impulsive, especially in dangerous situations like driving or being on a ladder, which I mentioned earlier. A few more examples of moments of regret for those of us with ADHD include:

- Needing to slow down and trying not to do everything so quickly.

- As a child, having accidents in your pants because you will not take time to go to the restroom.
- Saying the wrong thing when upset with your boss, school board, or friend.
- Driving without paying attention.
- Writing a mean letter, email, or text.
- Purchasing overpriced items on a whim.
- Making personal and professional bad decisions because you're tired.
- Getting tattoos, body piercings, haircuts, or hair dyes in the spur of the moment.
- Going to the grocery store and buying items you do not need or that are not healthy.
- Having sexual intercourse and thus having unplanned pregnancies only because you did not take time to plan.

By knowing we are predisposed to be impulsive, we can self-talk, use our superpowers, and even medicate ourselves to avoid costly or deadly mistakes.

Tips on Spontaneity

People with ADHD often struggle with impulsiveness. To me, impulsiveness is an uncontrollable form of spontaneity. Usually, the impulsive action is one I'm trying to avoid or limit. We can't always be successful in that endeavor, so here are a few of those situations and what I do to curb the impulse.

1. Impulsive eating has caused me to eat all hours during the night, snack on bad food, eat when I am not hungry, etc., which can lead to significant weight gain.

    What I Do:

    Every time I eat, I ask myself, "Am I really hungry or just bored?"

    I ask myself, "Have I been drinking enough water?"

    I tell myself I should not eat after 6:00 p.m.

2. Impulsive driving mistakes have led to car crashes and many other vehicle problems.

    What I Do:

    I self-talk about bad wrecks and how much I enjoy life.

    I try to leave early for every event I attend.

    I tell myself to have restraint from taking chances, especially those that can impact my way of life.

    I do a quick worst-case scenario thought process before taking that chance on passing someone, speeding, or any other risky maneuver.

3. Impulsive thoughts have led me to interrupt people when they are talking.

What I Do:

The whole time someone is talking to me I tell myself to pay attention to what they are saying. If they tell me their name, I repeat it over and over in my head and try to think of someone I know with the same name. I constantly tell myself to wait until they finish talking before I talk. If I do interrupt, I tell people this is a bad habit that goes along with having ADHD and I'm interrupting because I am afraid of forgetting what I am going to say or I am just excited about the conversation.

4. Impulsive decision-making within a group context can be challenging when I'm off and running with an idea before I fully explain it to the group or get them on board with the idea. Thus, even good decisions do not work without taking the time to sell people on the reasons for the decision.

What I Do:

Constantly remind myself that people support what they help create. Great leaders build up other people to become leaders. Remind myself that the best decisions will not work unless a lot of people want the decision to work.

Superpower 11

Compassion

We know that most people with ADHD are compassionate. If asked, almost everyone will say they are compassionate, ADHD or not. Some will try to give an impression of compassion and still others are compassionate but try to hide it. There is no doubt my children and I are very compassionate human beings. I believe this superpower stems from ADHD individuals being picked on and even humiliated as children. Many times, in our youth we just do not fit in and do not have the social skills to disguise it. We know what it is like to have people think they are better than us, make fun of us, and lose patience with us for being late, not understanding things, making mistakes, or getting off topic. These are the "symptoms" of ADHD that fuel the superpower of compassion.

Compassion in My Personal Life

Often, we struggle to make friends early in life. I know what it feels like to be the underdog, so I have a soft place in my heart for those who are less fortunate. Those of us with ADHD have had to work hard to overcome challenges, making us especially drawn to those in need, whether it is emotional support, helping improve others' lots in life, or sticking up for someone who's being picked on. I choose not to be around people who are mean to others. Have you ever been to a restaurant or in a checkout line when a customer is being rude to the waitstaff, server, or clerk? In several circumstances, I have opened my can of spinach and stepped in to help those in need. I see that clerk or waiter as myself working summer jobs to earn a little money. Or I see the person being heckled or ridiculed as my child. One time I did not get involved and ended up mad at myself for not intervening. While I may not always be confrontational, I will always try to put the person being abused in a good mood after the moment has passed and the negative person has left.

My children feel the same way. I was so proud of my son when he told me he quit being friends with a college teammate after they went to a restaurant and this teammate made fun of the waiter. Like my son, I would never allow someone to mistreat a person giving us service. I never want to be associated with anyone who treats others in that way, and I have my ADHD superpower of compassion to thank for it.

I love a good underdog story. One of my favorites is *Rocky*. Those who are familiar with Sylvester Stallone know that he himself was down and out and the original *Rocky* film made him a star. It was an underdog becoming successful with a movie about an underdog.

I mentioned earlier that my daughter, Erienne, also has ADHD and is a nurse. The medical field is a perfect profession for the compassion superpower. She often tells me stories about her patients. I can tell she really cares about them and makes great connections with those under her care. Her first nursing job was working with elderly patients. She would come home talking about them as if they were her extended family. She would check on her patients and stay with them even when she was off the clock. I have been with her several times when she received a call that one of her patients had passed away. Immediately her mood would become somber, and I knew it would bother her and be on her mind the remainder of the evening. Often, she knew when patients did not have family and she became the surrogate relative for these individuals. The time she spent in that position made the lives of her patients much better during their last days. We would all be very fortunate to have my daughter as our nurse. Today, she works in a neonatal intensive care unit continuing her trend of helping those in dire need.

Compassion in My Professional Life

I was interviewing a very popular high school student who was diagnosed with ADHD. During the interview, I asked her why she was so popular among all her peers. Without using the word *compassion*, she discussed how she keeps items in her purse to take care of her friends. She told me about one friend who has headaches, so she keeps Tylenol for them, one friend is always getting injured, so she always has Band-Aids and ointment for her. She is also the friend everyone tells their problems to, and she tells me specific stories about how she listens and then gives relationship advice. At times I felt as if I were talking to female version of me.

Communicate the Tendencies and Idiosyncrasies of Your Superpowers

Be up front. I believe communicating that you're a fallible human being is a good thing. I've found showing vulnerability helps build relationships. We have ADHD and our idiosyncrasies are not for everyone. Wouldn't you rather be yourself and be liked for your true self than a false self you present to be more attractive to potential partners?

Failing to communicate your tendencies means you are living in hiding. Delaying telling your partner may bring conflict down the road when they see the ADHD behavior you were trying to hide.

My son, Russ, hates to waste time looking for items, but his method of organization is totally different than mine. At age thirty, Russ decided he was going to come to my house and work a few weeks from my home office. The stories of the two of us together under the same roof would make quite a book by itself. On this visit, Russ entered my house and within one day he totally messed up three of my nicely organized rooms. I initially did not handle this very well as I grabbed all his stuff (clothes, drinking glasses, half-filled bottles of soda, etc.) and took everything to one room—his bedroom. I yelled at him that I was only going to allow him one room to destroy during his stay. One thing that is great about both of us knowing we have ADHD is that we can tell when one of us has become unhinged so the other knows to remain calm. Later, after the storm passed and I was calm, I asked him to explain why he threw his stuff everywhere. He explained that keeping his stuff out in the open allows him to see anything and everything when he needs it.

While I could never live that way and I feel sorry for his wife, at least now I understand his line thinking and his coping strategy. I still told him he could only be messy in his bedroom and adjoining bathroom, but the rest of my house will be done my way. By talking with our loved ones about our superpowers and idiosyncrasies it will help all involved have a better understanding and more compassion about why we do what we do.

As a teacher, I could relate to students very well. Over the years, I built a reputation among students as being someone they could trust. By the time I got out of teaching, I was a very popular teacher. I really enjoyed being that teacher that kids would come and talk to before and after school or at lunchtime.

When I began my teaching career, each year I had one freshman class that had several students who were not on a college track. I struggled initially with this group until I learned to just slow down and get to know them. I had extra compassion for this group of kids because I could see myself in them. This one group of boys in my class wanted to start a window tinting business. I told them if they worked hard in class for me, I would hire them to tint the windows on my car. Well, they held up their end of the bargain, so I hired them. Their only problem was that they did not have a place to conduct their business. So, I allowed them to come to my house where I fed them, and they tinted my windows. Even though they did not do a very good job, I bragged on them like crazy. These boys would always come to talk with me at school, at after-school events, and if I ran into them in the community.

I remember other teachers told me I should have never let these kids come to my house. They thought these kids might steal from me someday and I just said, "We'll see." That Halloween, many teachers in my neighborhood had their homes vandalized with paint, eggs, and toilet paper. My house was the only home in the area that was not touched. I can't be sure, but I believe the window-tinting boys were the culprits and decided not to target my house. I always like to say if kids know you care about them, they will protect you.

will.i.am is a rapper, producer, and actor who became famous as a member of the hip-hop group Black Eyed Peas. He's not shy about speaking about his ADHD. Regarding not being able to sit still or concentrate on one idea, he says, "Those traits work well for me in studios and in meetings about creative ideas. I've figured out a place for it. If you listen to the songs I write, they are the most ADHD songs ever. They have five hooks in one and it all happens in three minutes. I figured out a way of working with it."[38]

Years later, I had compassion for a group of boys in my class who wanted to start installing car stereos. I made the same deal with them as I did with the window tinters, and they came to my house and installed the stereo. One day, while I was on outside lunch duty, the police pulled up and asked to see me. Sure enough, these kids had installed a stolen stereo in my car. I had paid good money for this stolen stereo. I just laughed it off with the students and refused to press charges. One of the parents coordinated the efforts and repaid me. I joked with these kids about it during their entire time in high school.

I have always found it easy to relate to students and have compassion for them. Maybe it was a result of growing up in the projects with ADHD and only being able to improve my circumstances because I could put a ball through a hoop. I believe schools exist for students and somehow, while everyone echoes that sentiment, our schools do not always function in that light.

Tips on Compassion

Here are a few situations I encounter with my compassion superpower and a few tips on what someone with ADHD can do. I'd like to also point out it is much easier to write down tips than it is to practice them. It is only by knowing our tendencies and using our superpowers wisely that we have a chance to prevent very costly mistakes that can last a lifetime.

1. I've found that being compassionate leads people to try to take advantage of me. In leadership, some people will want to be my friend so they can win my favoritism or at least never have to worry about being fired.

   What I Do:

   As a supervisor, I keep some distance with all employees as it makes personnel decisions so much easier.

2. Some people will bring me all their problems both personally and professionally. These people will test everyone till they find the compassionate ones, which many times are those with ADHD. In public school systems in Kentucky, teachers receive ten sick days a year and they can donate their sick days to other employees. In every school district where I worked, there were teachers who really needed the extra sick days but there were also a couple of teachers that used their ten days and would go around and beg for more days. They did it every year and they would always find some new teacher that would give them extra days.

What I Do:

Find out about the history of the person. Ask others if this person always has problems or if they might really need help. Investigate before action. Also, remember not to be the knight in shining armor galloping to rescue the damsel in distress. I can be prone to entering relationships with people because they sense my compassion and will prey on my superpower, hoping I will come to rescue them.

Superpower 12

Hopeless Romantic

"If you find someone you love in your life, then hang on to that love."

—Princess Diana[39]

Relationships are hard even in the very best of circumstances. That said, just like having to work harder than our peers in school, those of us with ADHD may also have to work a little harder in our romantic relationships. During our middle and high school years, we tend to have some social awkwardness and may not be quite as mature as others of the same age. As an educator, I've noticed that boys are often about two years behind girls their age. For boys with ADHD, the gap can even be wider.

I have always been a hopeless romantic. Having a girlfriend and being successful in relationships were always important goals in my life. However, those of us with ADHD do get bored easily, which is one reason many people with ADHD do not have long-lasting relationships. It is critical that we are aware of our tendencies that may not be conducive to long-term relationships. If we are self-aware and up front about our characteristics and tendencies with our partner, we increase our chances of creating a deep, lasting bond. I try to self-talk and apologize whenever necessary. I also tap into my hyperfocus superpower so I can more deeply engage with my partner. I believe most people are attracted to fun and spontaneity, which we tend to have in abundance. I would recommend to those who choose an ADHD partner, buckle up and hang on as it's going to be quite a ride!

Meeting Amy

Later in life, as I learned how to tap into my superpowers, my relationships blossomed. During social occasions, I became the fun person and at times I felt the pressure that others even expected me to change dull moments into once-in-a-lifetime memories. People also seek out my ideas to organize parties, although *planning* fun is not really in line with my spontaneity superpower!

Public Service Announcement

As you know, I am a proponent of medication. I believe there are millions of older folks with ADHD that could really benefit from medication. It will make you less anxious, better in your relationships, and could possibly save a marriage where ADHD behavior is causing tension. My life became much easier the first time I tried ADHD medication at age fifty and I can say without hesitation that because of Adderall, these are truly the best days of my life. It is not just me—I have talked with many others who became medicated at a later age, and they all say something similar. I know that I am so much better with dating, friendships, marriage, jobs, etc. After I had been on medication for about a year, I called my ex-wife just to apologize for having to put up with my untrained ADHD brain. Being the wife of a man with ADHD, along with having two ADHD children, had to have been very difficult at times. To this day, my ex-wife and I are good friends, and we still get together for family functions with Amy and the kids. We all generally end up laughing at the plethora of funny stories and situations that only two different spouses of an ADHD person could tell. I am usually the butt of most of the jokes but also know I deserve everything they dish out. I know my children appreciate all of us getting along so well.

I became single later in life, and for a few years, I joined a couple of dating sites. I had a blast and believe the ladies I dated enjoyed our time together. I became hyperfocused on having fun. First came my profile. I wanted my pictures and my bio to show fun and a zest for life. I made everything a competition as it stimulated and focused my brain. I made a game out of trying to get prospective dates for a lunch or dinner meeting. When out on a date, I tried to be very engaging and make the date fun. I wanted to be romantic! I always wanted the person to like me regardless of if there was ever going to be a follow-up. I know this is not going to endear me to readers, but I wanted the person to want to see me again. If I failed to get a follow-up date, it really bothered me, and I would reflect on what could have gone wrong. What can I say? My competitive ADHD nature was in high gear.

There is no doubt in my mind that fun breeds attraction. The person with ADHD who can demonstrate fun and spontaneity on dates can be very successful on the dating scene. I also made it a competitive game of getting my date to talk more about themselves than I talked about myself. I have to self-talk during the date to make sure I do not interrupt and that I am a good listener.

At times, I was seeing three or four people a week and there were very few dull moments. Thus, my brain was getting plenty of dopamine and I was content. I have to admit there were down days when it was not fun being alone and it was a little harder keeping up at age fifty. People would always tell me that I would eventually find that one person and I scoffed, asking, why would I want that? Then I met Amy.

I remember one Sunday waking up with no one beside me and being a little mentally tired. The Cincinnati Bengals happened to be playing and none of the ladies I was seeing were able to watch the game with me. Out of options, I threw a Hail Mary—I visited a new dating site that I had paid for but had never used to find a date. When I saw on Amy's profile that she enjoyed watching the Bengals play, I thought she could be a good companion for the game. Not only did I find her attractive, but she also had lots of fun pictures on her profile. My message was simple and clear. "I must meet you and I would love to watch the Bengals play this afternoon."

Amy agreed to meet at a sports bar and from the very beginning I had a feeling this was going to be different. She told me her account was going to expire in three days and she was not planning to renew it. She had not had very good experiences using a dating app and I could tell by her initial body language she was not expecting this date to go well either.

To make matters worse, we quickly discovered that we had nothing in common. I told her I was just looking to have fun and not get serious with anyone. I also told her I had not read much of her profile . . . I just liked her pictures. She did not like those comments and considered that quite shallow. She told me she had very high standards and most men could not pass her "test" anyway. As I began to finish my drink and end the date, I realized she had knocked me off my game and I had not used any of my superpowers. She even got me to talk more about myself than she did. Now my competitive nature came out. I thought, *I am going to get this lady to like me.* As I took the last sip of my drink, I said, "Even though we have nothing in common, I want to hear about your 'test.'" I then said, "It's a shame we are so unalike, as with our two jobs, we can do anything in this world we want to do." I knew that last piece at least would bide me a little more time. She then threw out her test to me.

1. Pass the "social engagement test"—She attended major functions for work and needed a partner who could socialize with high-ranking officials.

   I was feeling pretty cocky, so I said, "I know you already know that I am a school superintendent in charge of a thirty-million-dollar company, I have written five books, and I am a national presenter. I have this one."

2. Pass the "friend test"—She had one friend she really trusted, and that friend would go out with us and later give Amy her opinion of me.

I also liked my chances with this test as I knew I could turn on the charm when hyperfocused.

3. Pass the "brother test"—Both her brothers were in the military and loved spending time with their sister. They shot clay pigeons on weekends.

    I was not as confident with this test. I was nervous that Amy's brothers were going to see me as a person who was going to steal their sister's time away from them. Plus, I had never shot anything in my life.

After Amy listed several more tests, I stopped her and said, "No wonder you are single!" This caused her to crack a smile. I could tell she was not used to directness as she probably intimidated a lot of men. Still, I got the feeling I was wearing down her defenses. Even though we both thought this would be our first and only date, it seemed like we were at least starting to enjoy our time together. I realized we had not even been watching the Bengals game.

It was at this moment I decided to do something crazy, and it would either make or break this entire evening. After all, I was seeing other women at the time so why not? Still talking about her tests, I asked her at what point was the sleeping together test? (I actually used the "F" word.) Amy backed up as if she were leaving and then leaned back over the table and said, "After you meet my mother." I thought that was the best possible answer and delivery she could have given me. I just started laughing and we then ordered dinner.

After two and a half hours of battling—as we were both acting as if we were conducting a job interview—we said our goodbyes without ever watching the game. I went home exhausted and went straight to bed.

Two weeks went by and no word from Amy. I was very confused because I thought I did really well on the date and we both seemed to have a good time. I started to think she'd never call and found myself disappointed. You can imagine how my face lit up when out of the blue I saw her name come up on my phone. There would at least be one more date. In my own competitive mind, I told myself, *I've still got it.*

I believe my superpowers of being spontaneous, risk-taking, and hyperfocus are some of the reasons why Amy eventually called me back after our first meeting. Had I not known how to use my ADHD superpowers, I would have never been able to make it through my two-and-a-half-hour job interview date.

Knowing what we want and being able to tap into our superpowers is an advantage we have over those without ADHD. Using my hopeless romantic superpower, I became hyperfocused on Amy and I was determined to make her like me.

I made sure our next date was fun, as I chose an exciting bar during a big game. I then chose a fun couple to join us. I also wanted Amy to see me in my suit, so I had an excuse to still have it on after work. Finally, I decided I would not even try to kiss her until the third date or after.

The next date I scheduled at my home with the same couple. I personally cooked for everyone and had everything very well planned. My house is always clean but, on this day, it was spotless. After the meal, we sat outside, listened to music, played cards, and had a really fun evening.

For Amy's second test, I met her friend at a trivia night at a bar. Knowing I was not that good with trivia, I had a few teachers in my school system who were seasoned trivia players, so I asked them to come and be on our team. We won the contest—the only time Amy and her friend had ever won at trivia night. Needless to say, I made the night about her friend and passed the friend test.

Every date was well planned, while always leaving room for spontaneous fun. On our fourth date, we ended up watching an old romantic comedy called *Three Coins in the Fountain*, which took place at the Trevi Fountain, also called the Fountain of Love, in Rome. After we watched the movie, we planned a trip to Rome together. I should clarify that *Amy* was the one who suggested the trip. I was blown away that she'd suggest something so bold . . . something I would have done! She wasn't bluffing either. She actually pulled her laptop from her backpack and scheduled the flights right then and there. It really endeared her to me. We had only known each other for about a month and now we were going to Rome?

The next week I said, "Since we met watching a football game, I want to go to Las Vegas to watch the Super Bowl." She agreed, so we planned that trip. During this time everyone thought we had lost our minds. Both her brothers and my family thought we were moving way too fast. But my ADHD hopeless romantic superpower told me this was going to be an amazing trip with someone I just knew was a great fit for me.

I knew Amy liked the outdoors, so when we got off the plane in Las Vegas I surprised her by saying I had rented a Jeep. Then, instead of going to the hotel, I had arranged for us to go to an off-roading area where we could drive up on top of the hills outside of Vegas. She was very scared when I went off-road as she knew this was out of my expertise. She even yelled at me to put it into four-wheel drive.

We then went back into the city, made all kinds of bets on the Super Bowl, went to a marijuana shop, attended a Super Bowl party, won a lot of money on our bets, and overall had a great time. It was a crazy couple of days. It had only been two months since this woman was ice cold to me at our first meeting, and now we were in Vegas having a blast.

Then, on the last day of our trip, we were riding around in our Jeep, and she looked over and asked me to marry her.

I was caught off guard in that moment. I had been thinking that when we went on our Rome trip later that summer if all was still going well, I might ask her to marry me at the Trevi Fountain, from the movie. So, I told her no as nicely as I could, and it did not go over well at all—Amy had really put herself out there and she was not used to being told no. The mood in the Jeep immediately had become ice cold. I would be lying if I said I didn't want to say yes, but the hopeless romantic in me really wanted to get down on his knees at the Trevi Fountain.

Still, we moved on from that moment. During the next month, we watched one of my all-time favorite movies, A Star Is Born. In that movie, Bradley Cooper makes Lady Gaga an engagement ring out of guitar string. The Rome trip was coming up and I had purchased Amy a beautiful diamond ring. Being afraid to take the ring to Rome, I found a person to make an engagement ring out of guitar string, which I presented to her later at the fountain in Rome. Luckily for me, she said yes!

I continued to tap into my hopeless romantic superpower, as we decided to elope to get married behind the Hotel Dell in San Diego. I had a few friends who just happened to be in California who stood up to be our witnesses. Then we came back home and had a big party with our friends and family as we rented the Purple People Bridge that connects Ohio to Kentucky. Yes, we actually rented the bridge. We rode in on scooters, said our vows, Amy sang to me, and we ate, danced, and had wedding cake on that beautiful September night!

> Jessica McCabe is a bit of an anomaly on this list. She's famous for her YouTube channel about . . . ADHD. Over one million people subscribe to her videos about her life with ADHD. She has even done a TED Talk about her experiences.[40]

Since Amy had asked me to marry her in Vegas and I had said no, I decided I wanted to renew our vows there the following year, so we flew our children and their dates to Vegas for the "wedding" as we called it. I was Elvis, Amy was Priscilla, and our kids all dressed up as hippies. The Elvis "wedding" was a lot of fun. The following year we had a beach "wedding" and the next we went to Tombstone, Arizona. We had fun events during the week like hatchet throwing, putt-putt golf, etc., and we always ate well. This celebration became so much fun that we decided to renew our vows every year. My son usually marries us each time.

Now, not every hopeless romantic gesture works out. Amy always said how much she loved horses, so I pulled some strings with a high-ranking government official to come up with two great Kentucky Derby tickets that placed us right at the finish line. I was so excited to give her these tickets. Well, it was a complete failure. When I gave her the tickets she said she's only into horse barrel racing. I had shown my ignorance as I just thought horse racing was horse racing. She is not from Kentucky and had no idea about the Kentucky Derby or the significance of those tickets. And, what's more, she had already made plans to be in the Cincinnati "Flying Pig Marathon" 5K race on that day. I was very deflated and gave back my Kentucky Derby tickets.

Every Christmas, I give Amy something with the Cincinnati Bengals on it. After all, had the Bengals not been playing on that one particular Sunday, we would have never met. We now have a lot of Bengals stuff all around the house—everything from footballs to chip clips. Sometimes on special occasions I take her to the restaurant where I had my two-and-a-half-hour job interview. I tip the host if they can give us our exact seats. I love doing random romantic gestures by sending flowers to her work for no reason or making unannounced lunch visits. I even send at least one love song or love quote to her each week.

While all this sounds like I am bragging, and it might be, I am making the point that if someone with ADHD decides they want to be hyperfocused on someone, they can be very romantic. And just like in all those rom-coms, like *Three Coins in the Fountain*, we are more than likely going to get the girl or guy.

Most of my dates after I began hacking into my ADHD superpowers were special. Long oceanside walks, musicals, sporting events, concerts, and cruises are all examples of trying to make dates as romantic and as fun as possible. My competitive nature is also at the root of this behavior. When I was young, my ADHD made sure no girl wanted to date me. Perhaps I still have that chip on my shoulder. We do have our issues and sometimes we come off as immature and sometimes we are even scared and intimidated by people we are attracted to. Now, with a fully trained ADHD brain and plenty of resources, I am able to tap into my hopeless romantic superpower.

Tips on Hopeless Romantic

- Only use your powers to do good.
- Finding your soulmate may be hard and you may get your heart broken . . . but it is well worth it.
- Know that your frustration with a partner may just be your ADHD boredom.
- Some people may not appreciate your ADHD superpowers and may not be a good fit. Don't take it too personally.
- Be careful and self-talk when you get angry. Some words cannot be taken back.

- Be very careful as we may attract users and people who do not have our best interests in mind.
- Be up front about your ADHD tendencies and talk about them.
- Remind others about your strengths/superpowers.
- Do not use your ADHD tendencies as an excuse.
- We may come across as more serious with partners and break the hearts of others. Since we are very empathetic, this also hurts us.

Calm Under Pressure

When those of us with the calm under pressure superpower are in a high-stakes or high-stress situation, dopamine is released in our brains, and we become calm when others around us are panicking. Because we have this ADHD superpower, you want us around when there is an emergency; you want us around when you hear a strange noise in the house or need to be rescued. We are wired for these situations. We make great emergency response professionals.

Calm Under Pressure in My Personal Life

From an early age, I was able to tap into my hyperfocus superpower in times of great stress and pressure. For those who are familiar with basketball, free throws can be more of a head game than a talent test. On the surface, one might not think a person with ADHD would be a good free throw shooter. After all, there are all these stimuli occurring with the crowd yelling and people behind the basket doing crazy things to get the attention of the shooter. One would think this would cause someone with ADHD to get distracted. However, despite those distractions, I happened to be a great free throw shooter (over 90 percent accuracy), and I always wanted to be the one shooting the free throws when the game was on the line. The stress of the late-game stakes actually relaxed me and activated my calm under pressure superpower.

Calm Under Pressure in My Professional Life

When my son was in high school, he played in the state basketball championship in Kentucky. It was a really big deal! As associate superintendent, I had put the team together five years prior. Having coached this team for so many years, I sort of felt like they were my team and I was so proud of my boys. I also played in this tournament in 1982 and lost in the championship.

My son's team had to play in the semifinals on a Saturday morning and, if they won, they would play that night for the championship.

The semifinal game was not much of a challenge for my team but there was plenty of drama. With thirty seconds to play and a sizable lead, my team started celebrating. A player from the other team undercut a player from our team in an attempt to hurt him. Our player fell hard on his head. One of the starters who was on the bench (our second-leading scorer) jumped onto the court at this egregious play. The ref called a technical foul on the player who jumped onto the court. The refs huddled up for about fifteen minutes and the crowd was wondering what was going on.

I knew very well what was going on. The rules state that when a technical foul is called, that player has to miss the next game. So, they were discussing whether they should make our player miss the championship game for going out onto the floor as a reaction to his hurt teammate. Frankly, the call was technically correct. The new rule was put into place to keep players from leaving the bench to fight. Yet, this call was not in the spirit of the rule, since our player was not fighting or even engaging with anyone on the other team.

After much discussion, the ref came to our bench and told our coach that he was calling the foul on the bench and not specifically on the player in question. After the game, I approached our coach as I wanted to know the call. I remember saying there's no such thing as a bench technical but was pleased that one of our key players would not miss the championship game and his last high school game. I thought to myself, *There is an example of a referee using common sense.*

As I was walking out of the arena, the head of officiating said, "You know, your team caught a break tonight. That ref broke the rules." I said, "Well, it was the right thing to do," which I could tell he did not agree with.

> Dav Pilkey is a cartoonist, most famous for his young adult "Captain Underpants" books. As someone who writes about child superheroes, he has spent a lot of time thinking about what makes each person special. He says ADHD is his own superpower. He even created the characters in his books during his time-outs in the hallway in second grade! He says, "I think one of the reasons why 'Captain Underpants' has resonated with so many children is because of the two boys that star in the books, George and Harold. They're always using their imagination . . . That's kind of an attainable superpower that we can all have."[41]

Right before the championship game, I received a text from our coach that our player was, after all, going to have to miss the game. The top brass of officiating had all convened and decided to change the referee's decision.

We had no time to practice, game-plan, or mentally prepare for this change. When our team heard our player would miss the championship game, they were outraged. Many were crying and felt we had no chance to win now.

Now my ADHD superpower kicked into action. As associate superintendent of the school district, I rounded up our principal and athletic director and together we approached the leadership of the tournament. Even though I was furious inside, I didn't show it and kept my cool. That allowed me to think on my feet and I asked the committee, "What's your plan? We're going to contest this decision and there won't be a game tonight. Do you have an evacuation plan for sending twenty thousand people home from the arena tonight?" I told them I had my story ready for CNN and I suggested they get moving on their plans.

The officials bristled and were shocked to hear my scheme. They replied that I'd lose my job if I did this. I was prepared for the committee's response and didn't back down. To convince them I was serious and put the pressure back on them, I said, "I'm going to go upstairs to talk to the media covering the event to tell them we are not going to play." My leaders whispered to me that I was crazy for deciding not to play, but I reassured them I fully intended to play. I explained if our bluff was called, we'd skip the pregame ceremonies, but we'd play after all if it came to it.

The lead committee person for the tournament put his hand on my shoulder and said, "We're going to try to work this out but just hold on. Do not go upstairs and talk with the press." So, to keep the pressure on them, I went courtside and stood by the radio station tables and told a few stations we might have a story for them. Well, sure enough, the committee contacted the referees to discuss the call that was made earlier in the day on that technical foul.

I didn't end up saying anything else to the radio stations because, just before the game started, the committee again reversed their decision, and our star player was able to play. We ended up winning the championship game and my bluff paid off. Our team was able to rally around having our star senior play in his final game. I'm thankful I was able to keep calm under pressure to ensure the player and the team were not wronged by an inflexible rule.

You may know Ty Pennington as the host of *Extreme Makeover: Home Edition*. He's also got ADHD. A self-taught carpenter and home improvement expert, he was able to channel his high energy in productive ways. "Once I figured out, I was pretty decent at art and people were interested in hiring me, I realized I had a skill besides injuring myself," Pennington says. "What's kind of funny is that I ended up working with power tools to pay my way through art school and still have all my digits."[42]

When I think of this story, I recall the moment that day when I was trying to figure out what to do about our player having to sit out the championship game. I remembered a bluff made in one of my favorite *Star Trek* episodes, "The Corbomite Maneuver," and it inspired my decision to see just how important it was to the commissioners to stick to a rule they knew wasn't in the spirit of the game. Captain Kirk always had these quick decisions to make. In the Corbomite episode, it looked like the crew of the *Enterprise* was going to be taken over by a hostile spaceship. Kirk said to Spock, "There must be something to do, something I've overlooked." Spock replied, "In chess, when one is outmatched, the game is over . . . checkmate." Kirk took a few minutes to think and then said, "Not chess, Mr. Spock, poker." Captian Kirk then announced to the attacking ship that he was about to release an explosive gas called corbomite that would blow up both ships. Spock and the crew looked at each other knowingly, seemingly saying to each other, "But there's no such thing as corbomite." The attacking ship decided not to destroy the *Enterprise* and risk being blown up in the process. Kirk had kept his cool and thought up a bluff that saved his ship and crew from certain destruction. Now that's calm under pressure!

Back in my early days as a school administrator, I had another situation that made me have to think on my feet. This may have been the hairiest situation I've been in. It was my first year as principal of a middle school. Lightning struck the building and the power went out for the entire school. The backup generator went out as well. Our cell phones weren't getting any reception. The school was a mostly windowless building and we had eight hundred kids and fifty teachers with no visibility and no way to communicate. While I was a little nervous, I could not show it in front of the staff or the students.

That's when my calm under pressure superpower kicked in. I grabbed a megaphone and communicated with teachers to make sure everyone was safe. I sent staff to locate flashlights for each room and formed a relay line with teachers up and down the hallways so that when I said something on the megaphone, they could tell the rooms throughout the school. I had to contact the central office and tell them we had to call off school for the entire district and get these kids home. We had to get them fed in the meantime, so I had staff go to the cafeteria to make sandwiches. We ended up being in that darkness for about three hours while administrators tried to coordinate getting the kids home. I truly believe that having a leader who doesn't panic and can jump into action and improvise on the spot like that helped us get through that chaotic day. I owe it all to my calm under pressure superpower.

Tips on Calm Under Pressure

We may take chances and unnecessary risks just to ignite this superpower. If we fail to save the day, people can get injured or worse. Being calm under pressure is not an invitation to take unnecessary risks. Let's say you are taking a group of people out for a boat cruise and get notified that a storm could be on the way. Try to self-talk and realize you are responsible for everyone's life, and it is not worth the rush you'd get for going out in dangerous conditions. Other examples are going outside to witness a tornado instead of taking cover or deciding to run with the bulls in Spain. While these may cause many people without ADHD to say, "No way!" our ADHD brains that stay calm in crazy situations may say, "Let's go!" Remembering to take calculated risks is essential with this superpower.

- Before throwing myself into a dangerous situation, I make sure I have contemplated less dangerous resolutions.
- Remember that while I may become calm under pressure, others will panic and may need my attention.
- Before I put myself in a dangerous situation, I ask myself: Is it worth it?
- Those of us with ADHD are predisposed to be the athlete who wants the ball in an important moment.

- We are the ones who will keep our composure while others are panicking. Find moments to be a helper for others.
- Our ADHD gives us advantages in stressful job opportunities. Look for careers where this superpower can be utilized.

Sense of Humor

When I was a child, it took me a while to learn humor. I laughed at jokes when others laughed but I didn't always get them. With ADHD it was hard for me to listen intently during the entire joke process. Maybe I wasn't really paying attention, or I simply didn't get the joke. So, even though I enjoyed humor at a young age, I really hadn't mastered it and I still have trouble telling a good joke without a lot of practice. During my presentations, it is much easier for me to play a funny video or tell a humorous anecdote. That's more my style of humor.

Sense of Humor in My Personal Life

My sense of humor came to fruition making creative basketball shots. I watched the Harlem Globetrotters as a kid and wanted to be able to do similar crazy and fun things with a basketball. I also enjoyed watching the late great Pistol Pete Maravich, the basketball trick shot artist. My teammates found my trick shots humorous, and it made me very hard to beat in the game H-O-R-S-E. Later in life, I had fun making trick shots for the players I coached. As a school leader, I always loved showing up at our basketball court and shooting basketballs with the players. These were silly, fun ways to connect with the players and students and I think these moments endeared me to them.

I enjoy sarcasm, and much of my sense of humor revolves around that style of joking. It is no surprise that both my children are very sarcastic, to the point where I was always afraid that they would get in trouble with their teachers in school. I think it's because I was sarcastic with them from an early age. I took my kids trick-or-treating for Halloween one year in our van. My daughter got her candy from one of the houses and, as she was getting back in the van, she tripped. At the same time, my son opened the door on the other side and my daughter fell right out *that* door! She was mad and embarrassed as she got back in. I turned to my daughter and said, "Great job, honey. I'm pretty sure this is the first time I've ever seen someone fall in and out of a car at the same time." As you can imagine, this only added fuel to my daughter's fire. To this day she remembers that moment. Now, many people do not get sarcasm, nor do they find it amusing, so I try to be cognizant of when I use it.

There's also a side of me that can see the humor in situations by connecting the dots that those without ADHD do not. This type of humor reminds me of *The Far Side* comics. Gary Larson, creator of *The Far Side*, makes connections between people, things, and situations that many wouldn't ever think of, which makes his comic strips uniquely funny. For me, this style of humor is another manifestation of my ADHD superpower.

Years ago, I went to the movie theater to see the fourth Jaws movie, *Jaws: The Revenge*. In the previews there was a G-rated movie with animals in it. One of the animals was getting mad in the preview, so I just quipped, "This time, it's personal" (which is the tagline for the Jaws movie). The room let out a big laugh as we all settled in for a fun theater experience.

Even though I'm not a great joketeller, my ADHD brain tries to find ways to inject humor into mundane or tedious situations. If I'm not laughing and enjoying myself, it's a pretty dull world. Listening to presentations is typically hard for me to get through because they are often boring. When I present, I like to include some humorous video clips to keep the mood light and to have fun with the material I'm trying to relay.

Cammi Granato is a gold medal–winning ice hockey player with ADHD. She has scored the most goals in U.S. women's hockey history. For many years, she struggled with organization, being undiagnosed at the time. As an adult, she went for testing, and when her ADHD diagnosis came back, things began to make sense for her. "I'd just assumed I wouldn't finish projects or return calls because I was lazy," she says. "Now I knew the cause, and could focus on solutions."[43]

I've got one story that really sums up my type of humor. I love fireworks and we like to light M-80s in summer, especially on the Fourth of July. Now, for some reason, I tend to end up in trouble on this holiday. My ADHD brain wants big booms and dangerous blasts. I don't shop at the roadside snakes and sparklers dealers; I go to the back rooms at fireworks retailers to get a secret stash of the good stuff.

My first wife's family was decidedly not into fireworks, let alone my illegal, backroom stuff. We were at their house for the Fourth of July and I wanted to inject some humor into the holiday. I saw some Barbies and Beanie Babies lying around, so my ADHD mind thought it would be funny to blow them up. The kids screamed with delight (or maybe terror) at the idea.

I had some huge bottle rockets that I wanted to set off. My wife and her sister were not into this idea, but the kids were intrigued by it, and they won out. My brother-in-law and I tied a doll to one of the bottle rockets in a big open field while our wives watched with crossed arms. We lit the bottle rocket and watched it go up. But I guess the weight of the Barbie doll made the rocket bend down and it started to come right back at us like it was the best boomerang in the world. Hell, you should have seen how fast the chairs and drinks went flying as everyone tried to run away. At that moment, when everyone was sure we'd all get burned and maimed, the rocket exploded, and sparks went everywhere right over our heads. After I knew no one was hurt, I cracked up laughing as there was just no way I could have ever made that happen if I had been trying. However, no one else appreciated the humor in that moment and I was greeted by a crowd of scornful faces. You'd think the family would hold a grudge after a stunt like that. But on the contrary, after the shock wore off, they began laughing right along with me. It turns out, they secretly always wanted me around because my ADHD sense of humor superpower brings fun and excitement to the party.

I may not have the greatest sense of humor, but I use it to make light of stressful situations and generally add some fun into boring, mundane everyday life. People seem to enjoy it, so I'm thankful for this ADHD superpower.

Sense of Humor in My Professional Life

I love using this superpower to inject some humor into meetings or professional situations. I feel this puts people at ease and relieves tension. But also, in a selfish sense, it makes meetings less boring.

When I received my lifetime achievement award in school administration, I invited a lot of people who helped me over my career, many of whom got up to tell stories about our time together. I soon realized that when most of these guests were telling stories about me, the stories tended to be about something funny that happened.

My transportation director, Joe, was a known prankster. He shared a story about the time I asked a police officer I knew to come to the school to accuse Joe of traffic violations as a prank. The police officer came into Joe's office, which was attached to my office. Several school leaders and I were able to listen through the door as the officer said they'd been getting complaints about Joe's bus speeding and running stop signs. Joe was incensed by the accusations, which he felt were not true. But we could tell that he was scared he was going to lose his job and worried about how it would reflect on the school system. Eventually, we opened the door and came in laughing. You should have seen his face when he realized we had pranked him.

Another staff member, Mark, told a story of an embarrassing moment he had one year. It was extremely cold and many of our students walked to school. When I was superintendent, I picked up a few students who were walking home from school and gave them a ride. As transportation director, Mark decided he would give students rides as well. He would just ask walkers if they wanted a ride and was just assuming all were students. Word got out that at one point Mark had mistakenly picked up a few homeless people and only realized it when they asked to be let out at the liquor store. After this story, I have had fun kidding Mark about how he gives great service to the *whole community*.

One way I use my sense of humor is to make myself personable to people. When we can be self-deprecating, it endears us to others. I took the opportunity to make a fool out of myself one time at a school employee banquet. My first wife, Mary, who worked at the school and was a great singer, was onstage speaking and said, as if on a whim, "Kelly, why don't you get up here and join me in a song?" Of course, the peanut gallery cheered on this idea, so I went up and we sang "I Got You Babe" together. It was brutally bad (at least on my part). The whole audience was on the floor laughing while I belted away, acting unaware. I'd accomplished my mission of making an ass of myself to everyone. I really think it showed my human, fallible side to our staff.

Now, fast-forward three months. I was at a movie in the theater when the sound went out. The theater staff had to stop the movie and figure out how to fix it. Well, wouldn't you know, way in the back of the theater someone yells, "Hey, Middleton, why don't you sing us a song?" I'm not sure which employee it was, but I can tell you by the laughs several more were in the theater as well that night. I just smiled as I knew I had left my mark on my staff by using my sense of humor superpower.

Tips on Sense of Humor

We tend to not listen well to others. Thus, we miss important points that need to be processed to understand a joke. We may then need to force a laugh to show the person we enjoyed the joke. Sometimes, I have laughed before the actual punch line was given. This is very embarrassing. I try to tune into people when they are telling a joke and not let my mind wander. Looking the person in the eye as they tell the joke and not letting anything distract me are also very important. This becomes particularly hard if there are others also listening to the joke standing right beside me.

I sometimes practice joke telling, including timing, or find other ways to be funny without telling jokes. I use funny true stories about myself and my life when I am presenting.

True life stories are easy to remember, and I can always embellish them if needed. I like to use funny video clips from movies and YouTube. Occasionally, I use pictures from the internet or my personal collection. I always set the situation up, show the picture or play the clip, inject some sarcasm, and then make it apply to the topic. Once we have a method for being funny, there is no limit to how far or high our fun meter can go.

- There is more to humor than just telling jokes.
- Our sense of timing may be a little off. Thus, we need to practice.
- I try to pay attention when someone starts telling a joke. (Self-talk)
- Humor can diffuse very stressful situations.
- People appreciate when leaders can laugh at themselves.

Superpower 15

Intuition

I was out with a friend one night when a lady came over and started flirting with him. I was watching them interact and I realized he wasn't picking up on the cues she was giving—playing with her hair, lightly touching him, and sitting close to him. It dawned on me that not everyone has the intuition to know when someone is hitting on them. I gave him a look to tell him (which he *was* able to pick up on) and he ended up getting her number and taking her out on a date. He later thanked me for the hint as I smiled to myself, happy that I was able to help a friend with my intuition.

This superpower benefits from the problem-solver superpower because thinking outside the box helps us make connections where others cannot see them. Similarly, people with ADHD see what those without ADHD tend to filter out, so we are noticing little bits of information others do not see or comprehend. Because of this extra information, we can pick up on what other people are feeling. I find myself regularly seeing through people's pretending to be happy or, on a professional level if I am at a board meeting, I can tell if someone has something they want to say but won't speak up. I can tell if people are nodding their heads even though they are not in agreement. I see body language and hear changes in a person's voice as I look for both verbal and nonverbal cues. I am able then to draw them more into conversations and, if necessary, provide more information to help them get to a better resolution. This superpower is essential for me when conducting group meetings and trying to get all members down the best path to solve important issues. I have also found that picking up on these cues makes people feel noticed, listened to, and valued.

Intuition in My Personal Life

People have joked that I have ESP or "Spidey sense." I usually can pick up on couples who are having relationship issues just by having dinner with them and observing their behavior with one another. I tend to hear a lot of people say, "Kelly, how did you know that was going to happen?" or "How did you know what I was going to say/ do?"

One important way I've been able to use this superpower is by listening to my gut feeling about people. This skill has been helpful in many ways but can also have an adverse effect. I can pick up on if one of my children is dating someone who is not a good fit. I don't necessarily voice this, because we all know how kids can sometimes like someone *even more* when their parents disapprove. I bit my lip when my son was dating a woman who just didn't seem like the right person for him. When he eventually decided he was going to ask her to marry him, I had to take him out to lunch to tell him my thoughts. I told him it was just my opinion and asked him to think over what I had to say. While this relationship did not work out, it had nothing to do with me giving him my thoughts. Often, people do not want to hear our intuitive thoughts and we just need to keep them to ourselves. Even if we are right, we might be wrong for sharing because, if we are correct, the person likely doesn't appreciate the "I told you so." In general, I try to resist the urge to say "I told you so" in any situation.

Intuition is an important characteristic of the best athletes. They need to anticipate what the other team and even their teammates are planning to do next. Quarterbacks, pitchers, and goaltenders must access intuition to be successful at the professional level. Using this ADHD superpower, in my opinion, gives us advantages over our non-ADHD peers. I certainly felt that I had a little bit of an advantage in sports as I somehow knew how the opponent was going to guard me in basketball. I could also see three shots ahead on the tennis court, allowing me to set the opponent up just how I wanted him. This is also why a lot of people don't want to play me in checkers or chess.

Intuition in My Professional Life

I've trusted my gut in many situations over the years. Because it's been right so often, I keep listening to my intuition. In the field of public school administration, listening to your gut can be a career-ender if you're not right. Furthermore, you simply can't wait for everyone to be on board to propose a change. I've also found the best changes are ones that aren't popular. So, listening to my intuition on an initiative is usually met with opposition and it puts massive pressure on being right. In other words, you'd better be sure about your hunch before you propose an idea. That's where my ADHD superpower has helped me enact change for over thirty years in my professional career.

Sometimes I think of the intuition superpower as an ability to see when someone has "it." That is, some feature or characteristic that you can't put your finger on but you have a feeling in your gut that they've got what it takes. I have interviewed hundreds of candidates for jobs at my schools. Many times, I can see someone's potential and ask questions that will confirm their abilities. While I have made my share of hiring mistakes, most of the people I have hired turned out to be superb fits for their jobs and have often exceeded our expectations.

Greg Lemond is a three-time Tour de France winner who also has ADHD. In 1986, he became the first American (and the first non-European) to win the Tour de France. Back then, not as much was known about ADHD. He says, "It was my kids who had shown stuff. ADD was just getting out in the news and the teachers recommended for one of my kids to go see a doctor for ADD. While they were getting examined, I read this 20-question questionnaire and I had every one of them and now I look back and I laugh about it because it explains a lot of stuff."[44]

When I was a superintendent, a parent once called me because her kid had head lice. She was livid because her child got lice at school and now had to do all the hard work of ridding her family and home of these little pests. Though unspoken, I could feel she was also embarrassed. So, I replied to this parent with a story about my own daughter getting lice at school—having to shave her head and throw away all her stuffed animals. (You can see in this situation I was using both compassion and intuition superpowers.) Once I finished talking about my experience with my daughter's lice, the mother's voice changed. I could tell she felt better hearing that I, superintendent of schools, had also dealt with head lice. We eventually got to a point where we were joking and taking the matter lightly. I was able to turn an angry parent around because I trusted my intuition about what she was feeling and where it was coming from. I've found people are often just embarrassed and need reassurance that we, as a school or school system, are not looking down on them. Having ADHD gives us a unique ability to walk in another person's shoes. If used correctly, the intuition superpower combined with compassion can really endear us to others.

I mentioned in previous chapters that I implemented a Move-Up Day at the end of the school year so students could visit their classrooms for the next year. Every time I proposed this (I've done so in three different school districts), nobody was initially on board with the idea. But each time, I had a gut feeling we could make it work. The biggest complaint was from staff who thought parents and families would complain about their students' future teacher. They also said it was too much extra work during the end of the year to institute a large-scale project like this. Some teachers cherished those last days with their students and didn't want to lose a single day with them. The end of the year is so busy, staff were worried about scheduling this day amid the other end-of-the-year chaos. Nevertheless, I went against popular opinion and pushed the initiative through.

Well, it turns out, my intuition superpower did not steer me wrong. After the first few years, I checked in with leaders and they reported that Move-Up Day was a huge success. Their fears turned out to be just that and they realized the initiative made the first week of school the next year go so much more smoothly. To this day, all schools and districts that implemented Move-Up Day still carry on this out-of-the-box tradition.

When it comes to making decisions, my intuition allows me to save time and get right to the heart of the matter: I can filter out all the other noise and see the big-picture questions. For me, those questions are: "Is it best for our students?" and "Is it legal?" If the answer is yes to those questions, I'll stand behind my decision regardless of any disagreement from others. In my personal and professional life, intuition is always giving me signals, thoughts, and ideas. More importantly, I know my intuition superpower has always got my back.

Tips on Intuition

Below are some challenges I've experienced with my intuition superpower and some ways I have dealt with them.

- When I know a course of action is right, I may move too fast without taking the time to build the necessary coalitions. Regardless of how sure I am the decision is correct, I must sell the ideas to others.
- I must still take time and take an idea through the change process. I have learned to look at a change process chart every time I get ready to make a big decision. Have I sold the appropriate people? Do we have the finances? Do I have an argument for the people who give reasons why it will never work?
- I have learned to build better coalitions or even allow others to think it was their decision. Some of these lessons come with experience, which also comes from doing change initiatives incorrectly.
- Having this superpower gives me an advantage when it comes to making long-term systemic change. Knowing our tendencies along the way also gives us a greater chance of success.
- Sometimes I just need to let people, including family, make their own mistakes. I cannot control everything. Sometimes I just need to keep my intuitions to myself.
- People never like it when I am correct and then I say, "I told you so."

Superpower 16

Personable

A school board member from a district where I used to work was celebrating a birthday and asked me to get together for dinner, even though it had been years since I had worked there. Does this sound familiar? Those of us with ADHD tend to make good impressions on people and are remembered as being people others like being around.

I like to think it's partly because I don't judge others. I've made so many mistakes, and done so many dumb things my whole life, I can be empathetic to people's issues and problems. Going into every interaction with that attitude, people pick up on it and feel more at ease. I seem to have an imaginary sign hanging over my head that says, "judgment-free zone." Combine that with the characteristic ADHD energy and fun attitude, and it's a recipe for friendship and being a person that others like being around.

Personable in My Personal Life

An old friend I hadn't been in touch with for over fifteen years once called me out of the blue to tell me he was leaving his wife. It felt like something very random and totally unexpected so I asked him why he chose to tell *me*. He said, "Well, I know you've been there, and you wouldn't shame me or judge me for it." It seems even years later people still remember how you make them feel due to the personable superpower. I thanked him for reaching out and we had a long, heartfelt conversation about relationships. I'm glad he called me, and even though we aren't in touch all that often, I know that if something like this happens again, he'll reach out and we'll reconnect.

Audra McDonald, the six-time Tony Award–winning actress, and singer, made headlines with one of her award acceptance speeches in which she thanked her mother and late father "for disobeying the doctor's orders and not medicating their hyper-active girl and finding out what she was into instead, and pushing her into the theatre." Some found the speech to be condemning medication, but McDonald later clarified that she was happy that her parents did what they did, as it was simply the right choice for her. Whether someone uses medication or not is a hard and personal decision.[45]

I've mentioned previously that being the life of the party comes naturally to many with ADHD. Being bored is one of our worst nightmares. I'm always thinking of new adventures, projects, and ideas each and every day. Amy told me once that when we are around her family, she'll make excuses for me when I'm on my medication and not my usual chatty, personable self. This is one of the drawbacks of ADHD medication and one that I take into consideration each day.

When you can laugh at yourself and take a joke, it endears you to people. Having been the butt of jokes my whole life, I've learned to have a sense of humor when I make a mistake and to own my shortcomings. I'll even laugh along with others at my faux pas. Eventually those stories might even end up in one of my books or presentations.

You may recall one of the tests Amy put me through when we first met was to have her brothers meet me and give their approval. For that test, Amy and I met up with her two brothers at a gun club for a day of shooting clay pigeons. I'd never seen these clay discs before; in fact, I'd never even shot a gun. I had to put my ammunition belt on, but I had no idea how to do it. So Amy pulled me aside out of view of her brothers and showed me how to put the belt on. Total transparency—she put it on for me. She was trying to make sure I didn't look bad in front of them. When we caught up with her brothers, they asked what took us so long. I just said, "Well, I didn't know how to put the belt on, so Amy had to do it for me." They just laughed and I could tell that they somewhat respected me for owning the fact that I had no idea what I was doing and did not even try to fake it. These two brothers gave me tips and helped me throughout the day. I even told them about the bruises I had all over my body because the shotgun I was using had quite a kick to it. It really hurt every time I shot the gun the entire last half of the day! Later, Amy said this day endeared me to her because I wasn't afraid to admit to her brothers, who were in the military, that I didn't know how to use guns. Being confident and comfortable with our shortcomings really is a superpower and one that makes us more personable.

Personable in My Professional Life

All this work has helped me when interviewing for jobs. I always do research on those who will be doing the interview. In my opinion, relationships are the most important part of any professional career, and having the personable superpower has really aided me in my leadership positions. In fact, I believe this superpower gives me an advantage over other, non-ADHD leaders in the industry. In school leadership, there are hundreds of people I needed to interact with on a regular basis, so showing my personable side and using this superpower allowed me to work over twenty years in school administration, my final eight years as superintendent of schools, and, later, to be one of the top salesmen for BloomBoard. In fact, being personable is a major theme in most of my leadership books.

Blind Spot

Our ADHD superpowers may not help us in every situation and can even cause some problems to pop up. I try to be aware of my blind spots as much as I can. Here are a few of mine. What are your ADHD blind spots?

Ignoring Limits: I might push myself too hard and ignore my physical and mental limits. If not careful, I can have stress-related health issues, and my performance can decline over time. I must remember I am not doing anyone any good if I am sick and unable to work or be a good husband or parent.

Isolation: I may isolate myself and then end up facing challenges alone—this can lead to a lack of support or loneliness. As a leader, even though I might know the path, I need to take the extra time and include everyone in decisions as people support what they help create. Men tend to isolate themselves when stressed. A man with ADHD will definitely go to his cave when stressed.

Avoidance of Vulnerability: I may tend to not show vulnerability, which is an important part of human connection and personal growth. Vulnerability helps connect with people. People need to know we are human and we do make mistakes.

Difficulty in Accepting Help: I can be reluctant to accept help. I need to seek advice and guidance even though I already believe I have a solution.

One of the biggest lessons I learned from working in public education was that, because I was personable, my employees trusted me more than some other leaders, whom I viewed as being less personable. That trust led to being given the benefit of the doubt often. I've found people tend to give the benefit of the doubt and not get as mad at someone they like or know. One way I was personable was to have monthly roundtables with a group of employees who represented their peers throughout the district to hear their problems and how leadership could support them better. Sometimes it was things you'd have no idea about if you didn't talk to them like getting a printer hooked up to one of the computers or getting rain gear for bus monitors who escort elementary school kids from the bus into the school. I had similar monthly meetings with a group of students and a group of teachers.

I also think it's important to truly engage with employees. In public schools, there are days to celebrate teachers, cooks, bus drivers, etc. I generally try to make it a big deal to celebrate with these employees on their days. For example, I always spent time with our central office staff on Administrative Professional Day. My leaders and I even cooked steaks for our staff during Teacher Appreciation Day. Some leaders will simply show up to meetings or team-building events. I am going to participate and interact with everyone—just showing up is not enough. Whether it is playing cornhole with our classified staff or helping custodians set up or tear down the gym for an event, I am going to jump in, participate, and interact with our staff. I also tried to walk the halls of each of our schools each week, pop into classrooms, and watch schoolwide events.

Tips on Personable

- Those of us with ADHD are always seeking new thoughts and ideas, so I find myself asking people lots of questions about themselves. We're inquisitive! By naturally making conversations about other people, you'll win them over and make them want to talk with you more. I find that often these conversations end up going in unexpected directions and people end up telling me more and more personal information because they're so at ease and having fun talking with someone who does not judge them.
- I try to use self-talk during conversations. I say to myself: *Remember their names and the names of others*

that come up in conversation, or *think of some good follow-up questions to ask the person.*

- Before attending an event, I try to think about who will be there so I can call them by name. Having their names and faces fresh in my mind helps to not stumble to recall their names when I run into them.
- I also try to make eye contact and have good nonverbal body language.
- I look for topics we might have in common as I am always trying to learn new things to help me converse with others. I like to travel and thus I look for common locations we can discuss. I have become well-versed in many subjects and can at least talk on a surface level about many topics.
- Because of my tendencies, I have also learned to plan. If I am ever having a meeting with someone new, I try to use the internet to find out everything I can about the person or people who will be in attendance.

Sense of Fairness

Any type of injustice really bothers me, and after pouring through numerous research articles, I am now a firm believer that those of us with ADHD tend to have a low tolerance for dishonesty, unfair situations, fakeness, and people who think they are better than others. Now, everyone might say they feel the same way as we do; however, we might be more likely to do something about it when we are confronted with such behavior. We might speak up when someone is being rude to waitstaff or when a student has been wronged by a teacher. We will do so even if it causes us to get into trouble.

Sense of Fairness in My Personal Life

I can relate to feeling like I'm being treated unfairly. When I was in school, I always thought it was not fair that I had to work so much harder to study for exams and still make a lower grade than someone who never studied for the tests. I also recall being teased, judged, and punished when I was younger for ADHD tendencies I couldn't control like being fidgety, lacking social skills, and making absent-minded mistakes. Because of these experiences, and the compassionate superpower, I am empathetic toward people who are suffering.

Then there are the little injustices that are inevitably thrown at us like a red light that won't turn green. I catch myself asking why I have to wait a long time for the light to turn green when there is no traffic coming either way. Or just because I do not have the proper casino status, I have to wait in a long line while the Platinum status line has no one in it. Oh, and I cannot use the restroom in the first-class section of an airplane when no one is using it? Those of us with ADHD are very likely to consider or even act on these faux pas.

David Neeleman is the founder of JetBlue Airways. He's proud of his ADHD, saying he doesn't want to be like everybody else. His decision to forego medication is something he's passionate about, noting that the creativity and risk-taking superpowers are worth some disorganization and inability to focus. He adds, "I knew I had strengths that other people

> didn't have, and my parents reminded me of them when
> my teachers didn't see them. I can distill complicated
> facts and come up with simple solutions. I can look out
> on an industry with all kinds of problems and say, 'How
> can I do this better?' My ADHD brain naturally searches
> for better ways of doing things."[46]

My school's senior trip was to go to the 1982 World's Fair in Nashville. I was so excited about this opportunity, as I thought it would be so much fun. For students like me who didn't have the money for the trip, the school offered us jobs selling at the concession stands at basketball and football events or cleaning up afterward. I couldn't do any of these jobs because I was playing in the games. The school didn't offer me any other options to pay for the trip, even though they were aware of my family's financial situation. So, since I didn't have any way to raise money for the trip, I couldn't go. Here I am starring in the games that bring in loads of money for the school system—the same games that are giving the other students opportunities to work to pay for the trip—and I can't even go! How is that fair? To this day, whenever I see any memorabilia from that World's Fair at an antique shop, I'm reminded of that injustice. This story even informed many of my values in my future school administration roles. I wouldn't let something like this happen to a student on my watch, even if I had to make an unpopular decision. Every student should have an advocate who will fight for them if necessary.

In my very first high school football game, I played wide receiver and ended up catching three of the four touchdowns our team scored in the game. I easily had the best day of anyone on the team. At the end of each game, the coach would give out a Star of the Game award, which was a free sandwich at a local sandwich shop and a small plaque. After the game, I sat and listened as the coach announced that he was going to give the award to two players: the quarterback and the running back. Of course, these two kids were the sons of the athletic director and superintendent, respectively. I was flabbergasted by this blatant injustice, but I knew I couldn't say anything.

Twenty years later, I ran into the coach and said, "I had three great catches—how did you give the award to the superintendent's and athletic director's kids?" He just replied, "Kelly, you work in school administration. You know how it goes. I'm no dummy." I must admit I did not expect his candor and it did make me laugh, but I left the conversation realizing that non-ADHD people don't understand that any small injustice—whether perceived or in reality—bothers us on a much greater level than others.

Sense of Fairness in My Professional Life

This superpower gives me the strength to fight the injustices of the world rather than turn a blind eye to them as so many other people do. If used correctly, this superpower can help you make your home, your community, and even this world a better place. As an educator, this superpower propelled me to be a favorite with students because I made it my mission to do what was right for them. One time, we had a dilemma about where to hold the prom. The school wanted to have it at a nearby conference center to make logistics easier, but the students wanted it in their own gym. The principal decided to vote on it when the students were away and could not voice their opinions, so surely the vote went in favor of the conference center. I found out about this and went to the superintendent to say this wasn't fair. He allowed me to stick my neck out to fix it by insisting on a revote when all students could be present. This time, the vote went in favor of using the gym. Now, the teachers and school administration did not take this well, and I lost some allies that day, but I did what I felt was right for the students, who, at the end of the day, are the only ones who should matter in these situations.

One story I heard in the news was about an elementary school boy who got in trouble for wearing a particular hat on hat day. Each student had created a unique hat they wore to school to meet their pen pals in person. The boy had put those little green plastic army men on his hat and was suspended for a weapons violation. The principal said it violated the zero-tolerance weapons policy. According to the boy's mother, the eight-year-old wanted to honor those serving the country with his hat. Unfortunately, the school saw it differently and banned the hat the boy designed and suspended the student from school.[47]

Situations like these drive me nuts because they happen in schools across the country every day. My sense of fairness superpower can't tolerate decisions that needlessly penalize students because of leaders and teachers who don't use common sense with rules. In my previous book, *Competing for Kids*, I have a chapter entitled "Don't Do Dumb Things." It brought me great pleasure to highlight injustices to students in school systems across the country. Sadly, that chapter could have been an entire book and even that would not be able to include all the injustices schools perpetrate on students each and every day.

Tips on Fairness

Below, I've listed some of my tendencies with my sense of fairness as well as some of my tricks to combat them.

- I tend to get too involved when I think my loved ones have been wronged. I may act quickly without even realizing how it might impact me or them. Not making rash decisions helps in these situations.
- I try to keep in mind that those of us with ADHD are the types of people who quit our jobs because of one act of injustice by our leader. Knowing this and remembering that such a quick decision can be more harmful to me helps keep quitting in check.
- Sometimes I will get into trouble by standing up for a perceived injustice to someone else. Often, it's worth the fallout, but treating each situation independently is important.
- I suggest that any time we hear about an injustice, we take the time to fully research the situation. As we have all become more aware in the past few years, even the news is tainted by political affiliation. When you self-talk after hearing about an injustice, try to predict all of the outcomes of your next actions. We want to use this superpower to do good because, if used improperly, it can do more harm. Imagine the harm Batman and Superman could do if they used their powers without having all the facts.

Pete Rose was one of the most prolific hitters in baseball history, holding multiple records to this day. Like myself, he was diagnosed with ADHD later in life. Despite not knowing he had ADHD, Pete, like so many other great athletes, learned to use his ADHD superpowers to propel him to greatness. He is arguably one of the best baseball players to ever play the game and a childhood favorite of mine. Pete ended his career with 4,256 hits—more than anyone who ever played the game. While many baseball fans know that fact, they might not know he also owns the Major League Baseball record for most at-bats (14,053) and most outs made (10,328). In other words, he had to fail more times than anyone in MLB history in order to get the hits record. This is the definition of persistence! He also had to play in almost all the games each season, which adds to that persistence he needed to lead the league in hits.

Persistent in My Personal Life

The persistent superpower is a refusal to give up in tough times. This is a tremendous superpower for those of us with ADHD who have harnessed it. When I was younger, I remember a lot of things not going my way. It would have been easy to give up so many times, but I learned to stick with some of them to work toward getting a better result.

My success with youth basketball is a result of my mom teaching me persistence. In third grade, I was really into baseball and not interested in taking on any new sports. One day, the basketball coach told my mom he wanted me on his team. My mom was excited about this opportunity and signed me up. Early in the season, I told my mom I wasn't enjoying basketball and asked her if I could quit. She said I couldn't quit until the year was over. So, I had to stick it out for the season and, eventually, I would come to like it and then love it. I would find time to practice every day. Since I did not have access to a gym during the winter months, I would practice outside in the snow and ice. I also remember putting in long hours of practice on hoops that were attached to garages with gravel driveways and in grass yards with hoops attached to telephone poles. Basketball was going to be my pathway out of poverty. If you've read the other chapters in this book, you know just how big basketball became in my life.

Using the persistent superpower along with the hyperfocus superpower can be very helpful in accomplishing goals. Nothing frustrates me more than losing items, which is a common trait of those of us with ADHD, and it is a reminder that my brain is wired differently. I can be very persistent when I can't find something. I will tear the whole house apart and stay up all night to find it. Now this may be a bit of a time waste sometimes and I can cause quite a mess, but if there's something that truly needs to be found, you can count on me to not rest (literally!!) until I've found it.

> In 2023 I received the Lifetime Achievement Award in Northern Kentucky from the chamber of commerce. This is a big deal in my region. The award recognizes success throughout a person's career and beyond. I have to thank my ADHD superpowers for this award. I believe my resiliency helped me overcome challenges that would have made others quit their job or public education in general; my restlessness made me keep striving for more responsibility and better outcomes from our schools; and my persistence kept me in the field to try to do my best.

I've always had to work harder than my peers without ADHD, so persistence was needed just to do what others took for granted. Take, for example, studying for a test. What others absorbed in class, I only caught a fraction of, so I needed to study even more. In college I used to bring tape recorders into class so I could listen to lectures again and again. I took notes from the recording and still needed to cram just before exam time. It was because I had struggled already through all of life's challenges with ADHD that I could tap into my persistence to graduate high school and eventually graduate from college.

Dating is another example of something that required persistence. Many of us with ADHD struggle to connect with peers during our childhood and teen years. A lot of that social knowledge just doesn't come naturally to us. As a result, I fumbled through dating for years when I was younger. It was frustrating to see my peers with girlfriends or talking to girls when I struggled to make such connections. At times, I wondered what was wrong with me. *I must be very ugly or stupid*, I thought. But I had to stick with it by learning more, trying harder, and figuring out by trial and error what works. That persistence has helped me become more successful with dating and relationships as an adult. Later in life, when I began to figure out how to utilize my superpowers, relationships were never a problem.

I had to consider adding this next part based on the age of those who might read this book. I decided to err on being completely transparent. While Adderall, Ritalin, and other stimulants help me with developing relationships, they also weaken sex drive and sexual completion. I have had parents tell me that their sons no longer wanted to take their medication in their teen years, and they just did not know why. My first question is, did he begin a new relationship?

Persistent in My Professional Life

As a school leader, driving initiatives requires so much persistence. For example, we desperately needed a theater and a new high school cafeteria—both of which were not in the budget by a long shot. We discovered this tax initiative called the Double Nickel that would cover the extra costs. But many considered it a bad idea as it would require a vote to increase property taxes. Getting public approval for this would be a challenge because property taxes were already high and over one-third of the kids in the city didn't even go to public school—they went to private school.

In addition to selling the idea to the public, I had to convince the school board it was a good idea, which was a challenge because they are elected members and backing an unpopular tax could risk their seats come the next election. I knew they would receive phone calls from people who would fight the tax; therefore I would need to keep reinforcing how important this money was for our school in every interaction with our board members and at our board meetings. At times, I thought we might be better off nixing the whole idea. But there just seemed like no other way to get the money and I kept thinking of how much our students would benefit from these facilities.

As an added challenge, there were people going door-to-door with a petition against this tax increase. It took a lot of persistence for me to stick with it through these challenges. Besides my own resolve, I had to help develop the persistence of my board as well. We were so successful in convincing the public we needed this facility upgrade, people called and asked to have their names *taken off the petition*. The petitioners did not receive enough names and we were able to get the new tax approved; thus our students ended up with a state-of-the-art theater, gymnasium, cafeteria, and even extra classrooms. As a bonus, those school board members I convinced to stick their necks out for this tax, all got reelected, which further reinforced our hard work. When someone with ADHD has a cause to fight for, they can be very persistent and hard to beat.

Pete Rose is known for being a world-class baseball player and for being kicked out of Major League Baseball for gambling on games. He didn't find out until he was sixty-two that there was a link between the two—when he got diagnosed with ADHD. The same condition that made him a great player also made him predisposed to gambling addiction. He notes that his gambling got so bad, "In all honesty, I no longer recognized the difference between one sport and another." In Rose's book about his gambling, he says, "ADHD is an explanation, not an excuse." On the subject of medication, he says, "I'm 62 years old. Why would I want to get started with that now?" Now, I personally believe it's never too late to make a change, but to each their own.[48]

I've found that when it comes to an idea, there are always others who are against it. Often, the side that's the most persistent wins. As a longtime leader, I was involved in countless debates on new initiatives. Any new idea in public education comes with lots of bureaucratic hurdles and challenges. Many times, I lost the argument, but usually, my ADHD superpower of persistence wore the opposition down and we were able to make big decisions that benefited our students.

In the business world, I used my persistence superpower with my work as a seller of online master's degrees for teachers at BloomBoard. Making a huge career shift from public education to private business at sixty years old was a challenge. I had to learn many new technologies and systems that were very far outside of my comfort zone and my skill set. However, I was able to harness my persistence superpower to be one of the top sellers in the country for my company.

Tips on Persistent

- It is important to know when to be persistent and when we need to let something go. This takes knowledge of our powers and the tendencies that come with the superpower.
- Be aware of potentially dangerous situations where persistence can negatively impact your life. Think about the Pete Rose anecdote in the text box above.
- I mentioned in the Resilience chapter that we may stick with a task or relationship even when the writing is on the wall that we should stop. Listen to people you trust and self-talk about the issues that accompany ADHD.
- We may need to identify times when persistence is needed. For example, if I'm not motivated, I can give up easily on tasks. Sometimes I get bored with one activity and move on to another one that's usually more appealing, leaving the first unfinished. By the end of the day, I've left a trail of half-finished projects in my wake.
- It can also manifest in the opposite way. Getting stuck on a task, especially one that interests us, can leave

a to-do list completely untouched because of such a diverting task.

- Keep track of time on various interests and tasks. Always know when and where you give your time and attention.

Superpower 19

Coping Skills

A s I mentioned earlier with the Resiliency superpower, I've had to deal with making mistakes throughout life because of my ADHD. Adversity is a constant for many of us, so we learn and develop coping skills along the way. In this chapter I'll share a few of mine.

Coping Skills in My Personal Life

Self-talk is a very important coping skill. Interrupting is a major ADHD trait of mine that I work on. I am constantly using self-talk to wait my turn and keep myself from interrupting people. It's also a reminder for me to listen to the other person.

I also use self-talk a lot when I'm cooking. I often want to leave food cooking on the stove to quickly get something done. I'll try to squeeze in another activity in the middle of waiting for water to boil or eggs to cook. This often ends in burned food or worse!

Those of us with ADHD get bored easily and can be very impatient. I get frustrated and must self-talk when I am behind slow-moving drivers, especially if I want to pass these cars. I mentioned the danger of impulsivity when driving earlier but I wanted to go into more detail here. I must remind myself that I can't just pass when the person in front of me is driving too slowly. I must stop and ask myself, *Is there enough room for me to get by? What if someone is speeding beyond the curve in front of us? What about all the lives that will be affected if I make a bad decision? Am I just being impatient?* I have the ability to ask myself these questions to gauge the situation and decide what to do. Knowing about ADHD accident percentages, I was terrified when both of my ADHD children received their driver's licenses. I was overbearing about them be careful and wearing their seat belts. On occasion, if I would see them driving, I would pull them over like a police officer and check their seat belts.

One of my favorite self-talk moments is asking myself, *Do you have your wallet, glasses/sunglasses, phone, and keys?* I use that just about every time I stand up to leave the house or a restaurant. Sometimes I try to sing it. Even with this coping skill, if unmedicated I sometimes will still end up forgetting some of these items. However, I would be much worse off without using self-talk.

> Jamie Oliver, famous British chef, was diagnosed with ADHD as a child. His outlet for creativity and energy is the kitchen, but that's not all he gets from cooking. According to ADHD Foundation, Oliver manages his ADHD with a healthy diet. Something we may all want to try![49]

Sometimes these behaviors can be challenging for our families and friends. It's a big help when they are patient and understanding with me when I'm forgetful and not practicing my self-talk. I recently had to run back into the house three times before I had everything I needed while Amy just sat in the car. She said, "I knew you'd be back in and out a few times. I factored that in with our timing." Amy will either read a book or play on her phone while I go in and out until I say I'm ready to go. Since she asks me not to be medicated, I guess she takes some responsibility. Regardless, I love that she understands my tendencies and reassures me they are overshadowed by my strengths.

One way I cope with ADHD is to be highly organized. I hate to waste time and will obsess about my stuff being in order. Thus, there is a place for every item in my house. I just do not have time to waste looking for things. I become enraged when I lose something and have been known to mess up the entire house trying to find some little item that I could simply go purchase at a store. Perhaps my anger about losing stuff reminds me of a feeling that something is not quite right with me. I eventually will self-talk to myself about the positives of being different. I have learned to embrace my superpowers and just go buy items that I lose. However, I still get frustrated when an item of mine is lost.

I use the calendar app on my phone to remind me when I need to go somewhere, take a call, or run an errand. Using the technology we have nowadays is a big help for those of us with ADHD. Shared calendars, phone alarms, and even GPS-enabled tracking tags all help me stay organized and in control. I get *excited* when I come across new products that help me with organization. I tell others about my new organizational tools. Often, they just look at me like I have lost my mind, but these new discoveries truly are game changers for me. When I told my editor, Mike, about my new battery case that houses all the different-sized batteries I use on a regular basis, he didn't understand why I needed one. "Can't you just keep new ones in the drawer?" he asked. I told him when my TV remote runs out of batteries, I get so frustrated. I often don't have batteries on hand or keep them in one specific place, so I may run through the house opening all the drawers or be tempted to take them from something important like a smoke detector. I often found myself having to run out to the store to get batteries at the most inopportune times. Having a designated case that my ADHD brain now *wants to keep full of new batteries* takes the stress out of when my remote dies and allows me to make a quick change without having to turn the house upside down, take from somewhere else, or go out of my way to go to the store.

> Mornings are my most productive time. I try to schedule my most challenging activities for the morning hours both professionally and personally. As a leader, I wanted tough meetings to occur early in the day. I also held most of my serious meetings in the morning. Are you more productive early in the day or afternoons? Do you plan accordingly?

Another facet of the coping skills superpower is pre-planning for activities to cut down on wasted time. A major part of pre-planning is having all the necessary supplies and materials before starting the task. For example, when I need to mow the lawn, I'll start getting ready the day before so I can make sure I don't get sidetracked by problems. I check that the mower has gas. I'll start it up if it's been sitting all winter so I don't have a problem starting it when I need to get it done. I check the weed wacker to make sure the string isn't broken (it often is because many of us with ADHD tend to break things). When I'm sure everything is ready to go, I can rest knowing that the next day I can just go out and mow. Getting *all* my clothes ready the night before is another example of pre-planning. A stain or item that doesn't fit right can really hold me up when getting ready in the morning when I'm on a time crunch. I am also much more likely to finish a task if I can go right to the task when I'm not getting interrupted by these issues.

Having a party really requires pre-planning. When I have done enough pre-planning so that I'm confident that any forseeable issues have been addressed, then that opens up the spontaneity superpower to kick in, which is always fun for me.

Pre-planning isn't always just for saving time. It also helps me to be *on* time, especially when I'm driving somewhere new. I sometimes get lost not paying attention to road signs or the GPS so I always pad my times to account for these delays.

I make to-do lists that I number based on priority so I can make sure I get the things done I need to and don't get stuck on something little that doesn't matter. As I mentioned earlier, getting stuck on something is one downside of the hyperfocus superpower. I also use the list in case I want to go in full ADHD mode and work on all of them at the same time. Having the list to refer back to helps me keep track of my tasks and choose one that I feel motivated to do next. This method energizes me.

I know that starting on my to-do list early in the morning is best for me, as that's my most productive time. As the day goes on and evening goes on, my brain gets tired from working it all day long. It takes a lot of energy to self-talk all day!

Coping Skills in My Professional Life

The coping skills superpower also includes adaptability. In my professional career, I've had to adapt to various different scenarios. As a school superintendent, there is crazy drama going on all the time. I credit my coping skills for getting me through these high-stress work moments. Dealing with upset parents outside my office, staff mad about their evaluations, a student overdosing, and a fight between students—among so many other things—can all happen within an hour on the same day in public schools. Coping with that pressure and stress really tries my skills. But on most days, I've been able to meet the demands of the job in stride. Heck, I must admit I kind of enjoy all the mayhem because there's never a dull moment!

Adapting to different scenarios, especially high-stress ones, really activates the coping skills superpower. For anyone who worked in education recently, the Covid-19 outbreak was a perfect example. When Covid hit our state, the governor worked with our commissioner to close all schools. As a school district superintendent, we had twenty-four hours to figure out how we were going to educate students from home and feed them for an undetermined number of days. Needless to say, the stress level was high, and every minute counted. Right in the middle of total chaos, our school board chair called to tell me that she had received a complaint from a city official that one of our flags at a particular school was looking a little shabby and needed to be replaced. I thought to myself, *In a time of absolute crisis, you're coming to me about a tattered flag?* Without my coping skills, I may have said the wrong thing to our school board member or called the city official myself to let him know my thoughts. Neither would have been advantageous to my job.

In response to the sudden need to educate all our students from home, we made the quick decision to send iPads and computers out to all our students, give every family access to the internet, and develop a plan to deliver food to every home before the end of each school day. We were also communicating with our parents, staff, board, city officials, and the media. It wound up being months before students would return to school. Looking back, our reaction in this time of crisis was unbelievable. I can now admit that I actually enjoyed this leadership moment as my ADHD superpower kicked in and allowed me the coping skills necessary to thrive in this high-stress environment.

Tips on Coping Skills

- The other side of our high-energy superpower is learning to calm down and be a good spouse or parent when arriving home.
- I use my coping skills superpower to compartmentalize some of the emotionally challenging things I've seen in a day and not bring them home. On more than one occasion, my wife has reminded me I am not the school superintendent when I walk into the house.
- Our challenge is to identify when our ADHD prevents us from doing what we want to do and find the coping skills to work around it.

As I've gotten older, my coping skills have improved and have made situations that would have left me stressed or frustrated much easier to handle. I often think about picking up the phone and calling or visiting some people to just apologize for my past behaviors that happened before I discovered my coping skills superpower.

Superpower 20

Zest for Life

For me, each and every day is a new adventure to be embraced wholeheartedly. Each sunrise does not just herald a new day but inspires a fresh start to pursue new dreams with passion and vigor. When life brings those of us with ADHD to a crossroads, we will be happiest if we choose the path that provides us with the most growth and joy while providing the greatest benefit for others. We step boldly, live passionately, and cherish each moment with gratitude. For in this boundless journey, the heart that loves life never misses a chance to dance.

I say that because those of us with ADHD are going to live life to the max, and thus we are going to dance. (I mean this metaphorically. Not everyone with ADHD likes to dance!) I can't wait to get up every day. Many times, I wake up at 4:00 a.m. for no other reason than because I want to knock out a few projects before sunrise. We want to be significant, have fun, and live life to the fullest.

I'd like to point out that this is a superpower that many with ADHD may struggle with. There have been times when I certainly did not have a zest for life. When I was younger, before I knew I had ADHD, there were times when life was daunting, frustrating, and depressing. It wasn't until I learned to harness my ADHD superpowers that I started to hit my stride with life and embrace all the craziness that comes along with having ADHD.

Zest for Life in My Personal Life

My zest for life superpower makes me seek out novelty and spur-of-the-moment situations, allowing me to enjoy life much more than my non-ADHD peers. No one wants to be around negative or unhappy people and this superpower allows me to be someone that others want to be around.

> "I don't want other people to decide who I am. I want to decide that for myself."[51]
>
> —Emma Watson, actress with ADHD

My kids and grandkids enjoy coming over to my house because I make it fun. I bought my house with fun in mind as I wanted a place where others—especially family members—would want to come visit. Thanks to my ADHD,

I want my house to be a party place! I have an indoor and outdoor pool, sauna, basketball court, pickleball court, cornhole boards, giant Jenga, and a bar. We also made some trails out back for hiking and four-wheeling and put in a clay pigeon shooting area. The bar and pantry are always fully stocked with everyone's favorite drinks, and I keep fireworks on hand for after-dark festivities. Many of us with ADHD love to go from one activity to another, keeping everyone busy and happy.

Having a zest for life is helpful with making new friends because I'll more than likely say yes to their fun ideas. I have that "why not?" mentality, so when people bring up activities or plans that even they don't know they want to do, I always encourage them to follow through with them, and I'll be right by their side. I am also not afraid to be the first to try a new activity and risk being the person everyone can laugh at. After all, people have laughed at me my whole life—it's worth it for me to encourage someone to try something new or fun. Now for many, my philosophy may conjure up an image of the little devil on the shoulder of those who live a more reserved lifestyle, but I prefer to think of myself as a *really fun* angel.

We've all heard the stories about people on their deathbeds being asked what they would have done differently. And one of the most common answers is that they didn't live life to the fullest. People wish they had taken that trip, asked out that one person, spent more time with the people they loved. They wish they had not been so worried about what others thought. With me, my ADHD zest for life superpower doesn't allow me to say no too often. I am going to dance. Furthermore, if I am not embracing my zest for life, I'm bored and miserable and generally no fun at all to be around.

In 2012, Britney Spears was struggling with many facets of her personal life. She was also struggling with ADHD as a judge on the TV show *X Factor*. She had to get up and take breaks during the long hours of auditions and was not able to take any medication, per the doctor's orders.[51] In the following years, medication problems caused by her conservatorship's decisions have been cited as a major source of her troubles, especially according to her Netflix documentary.[52] The takeaway from this? ADHD medication is a highly personal and serious decision that has to work for *you*.

Sometimes when my wife and I are on vacation, at the casino, or wherever, people come up to us and want to hang around us. These total strangers often ask if we want to have dinner with them too. It seems people are drawn to that "seize the day" mentality.

Now, one downside of this zest for life superpower is that people begin to *expect* me to bring the fun. It can be a lot of pressure, especially when that expectation is put on me ahead of time. Since I love to be spontaneous, this type of expectation makes it a little harder to tap into my superpower. I've found it is important to remind myself, my wife, and others that I can't always just snap my fingers and create an exciting activity or spontaneously fun moment.

Zest for Life in My Professional Life

Having a zest for life also makes me a contagious motivator at work. As superintendent, I was often given the task of planning team-building events for leadership retreats. The people in charge of the retreats would always say, "We could do it, but we know it won't be as much fun." So, I'd have us play bocce, go bowling, or watch a sports game together. I also used my zest for life superpower to plan some interesting games like an Amazing Race–style game, a Dating Game to see how well we knew each other, or a Clue murder-mystery game. What really brought us together as a leadership team were these moments when we could engage in camaraderie and let loose. Creating happiness with laughs and smiles endears people to us and fosters a positive relationship, which then further endears them to us and makes them motivated to work hard for us. I've found that high-performing teams tend to spend time outside work together. Something as simple as eating meals together can really build team rapport. I once brought mood rings to dinner with a group of coworkers and we had fun looking at them throughout the meal, joking about how each bite or sip made us feel. It doesn't always have to be wild and crazy, just creative and fun.

One of the themes in all my books is the power of relationships. The zest for life superpower is a driving force behind my relationship-building. It's what has made me able to pick up the phone and go to dinner with coworkers I hadn't worked with for years and what allows me to make new friendships wherever I go. I use this zest for life superpower to be a better friend, partner, parent, grandparent, build a better work team, and be a better leader.

Tips on Zest for Life

- Not everyone wants to have a "really fun angel" on their shoulder goading them to do something. We need to be judicious about when we push people outside their comfort zones.
- I can make some people nervous or I may have too much energy for them. My free-wheeling lifestyle is not for everyone. I'm not someone who goes well with those who want calmness.

- Sometimes I'll spend money foolishly, or buy things I don't need, which can be hard for partners.
- The zest for life superpower can also lead us to do dangerous things. I try to always weigh the consequences of my actions when using this superpower.
- Seek out friends and life partners that get your superpowers and your ADHD tendencies.
- I like making bucket lists of things I want to do in my lifetime. That way, my zest for life can be channeled into activities I really want to do!
- When choosing a lifetime partner, make sure they have the same zest for life.

Closing

These superpowers permeate every facet of my life—from childhood, through adulthood, as a student, son, father, husband, grandfather, boss, coworker, and friend. We need to be in control of our superpowers, or they may control us. Let's learn and teach others about our superpowers so we can use them to our advantage and not let our ADHD tendencies make life more difficult for us. I've seen many people on YouTube detailing their struggles with ADHD. While I have struggled with it mightily my whole life—and at times been frustrated and exasperated by my ADHD tendencies—I also know there are lessons I need to learn in each of these moments. Understanding my own weaknesses and strengths allows me to identify situations where I need to self-talk or tap into a superpower. Despite the challenges of having ADHD, I would never want to give up my superpowers that come with ADHD.

It pains me to know that there is still a stigma with ADHD. Many people don't get the help they need—whether it's medication, therapy, self-help books, or programs—because they are afraid to admit to themselves or others that they have ADHD. It also pains me when people think they are too old to be medicated. I plan on living an exciting life until I take my last breath and I am so happy I started mildly medicating at age fifty. At age sixty, I seldom medicate but, like a security blanket, I always keep a bottle of medication near me. Sometimes my wife, family, and friends may need me to medicate, which is okay with me.

One of my goals in writing this book is to educate not just the person with ADHD, but those people who are close to them in their lives. It helps to understand the "why" behind our behaviors. When someone "gets" us, it creates a more harmonious experience and relationship. I hope you can relate to some of my experiences, superpowers, and tendencies. If this book has you thinking about your own superpowers and idiosyncrasies with ADHD, I have done my job.

For boys, at the very least, look for teachers who have young boys of their own and know how boys grow and develop. Educate your children's teachers about ADHD tendencies in both boys and girls and your children. Monitor your children's relationships with their teachers and constantly be in communication with the teachers. Educate the teachers on your child's superpowers and make sure there are activities that will stimulate these powers.

Encourage your children to participate in extracurricular and cocurricular school activities like sports, art, music, drama, and technology. Make sure there is time each day for some physical activity. Always talk about the importance of developing a positive relationship between the teacher and your child.

As they continue to grow, help guide them into future jobs where they can use their superpowers. Jobs that do not require much creativity or are not geared toward our superpowers will feel like a prison.

As a parent, I always made sure our son, Russ, had the latest technology in his hands. As a presenter, I hired Russ to go on trips with me to set up the technology I was going to use during the presentation. At a very young age he saved me several times. Currently at the age of thirty-three, Russ has his own technology company. My daughter, Erienne, always loved babies and was so good at taking care of others. We helped guide her into the field of nursing where she is flourishing.

If there is a possibility of needing medication, please give it a chance and find that Goldilocks scenario of getting it *just right* for you. To all of us with ADHD, look for lifetime partners who appreciate our superpowers. Some research will tell you that we are attracted to non-ADHD people and that is probably a good thing. If both partners have ADHD, even more communication will be needed, as it is going to be a wild ride! And always look for a partner who shares your zest for life!

It is my hope that you, my children and grandchildren, will read this book and realize that you are lucky to have your ADHD gifts and do not let others tell you anything differently. Those without our superpowers will always have trouble understanding. Find and seek out others who, like you, possess these powers. It helps to be around others who understand and have experienced what it is like to not only use these superpowers but also know what it is like to be in a world that tries to constrain us and make us feel like we have some severe disorder that needs to be fixed. Find others with ADHD, discuss with others how to self-talk and game the system, unleash your superpowers, live a great fulfilling life, and perhaps make a positive contribution to your family, your school, your community, this nation, and the world!

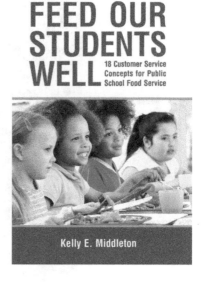

Endnotes

1   "Attention-Deficit / Hyperactivity Disorder (ADHD)." Centers for Disease Control and Prevention. Accessed May 10, 2024. https://www.cdc.gov/ncbddd/adhd/data.html

2   Wirth, Jennifer, and Harmon, Megan, "ADHD Statistics and Facts in 2024," *Forbes*. August 24, 2023. https://www.forbes.com/health/mind/adhd-statistics/#:~:text=An%20estimated%208.7%20million%20adults,continued%20ADHD%20symptoms%20into%20adulthood

3   Alejandro Jodorowsky, "Quote by Alejandro Jodorowsky," *Goodreads.com*, Accessed May 10, 2024. https://www.goodreads.com/quotes/650508-birds-born-in-a-cage-think-flying-is-an-illness

4   Landsman, Ian, "Why A Customer's Poor Planning IS Your Emergency," Helpspot.com, August 24, 2021. https://www.helpspot.com/blog/customer-planning-emergency#:~:text=It's%20a%20quote%20attributed%20to,%2C%20business%2Ddriven%20and%20otherwise

5   Inflow The ADHD App (@get_inflow). "Jim Carrey (@JimCarrey), Actor with #ADHD," Twitter, March 1, 2021, 6:18 a.m., https://twitter.com/get_inflow/status/1366347024803778561

6   Shire PLC, "Celebrity Dancer, Karina Smirnoff, Speaks Out for the First Time On How ADHD Has Impacted Her Life," PR Newswire, September 16, 2009. https://web.archive.org/web/20170520051354/http://www.prnewswire.com/news-releases/celebrity-dancer-karina-smirnoff-speaks-out-for-the-first-time-on-how-adhd-has-impacted-her-life-62186832.html

7   P.T. Barnum, "P.T. Barnum Quotes," *Goodreads.com,* Accessed May 10, 2024. https://www.goodreads.com/author/quotes/201036.P_T_Barnum

8   Mellon, Steve, "Can Terry Bradshaw Spell 'Cat?' The history of an insult," *The Pittsburgh Post-Gazette,* January 9, 2017. Print.

9   Dowd, Kathy Ehrich, "Michael Phelps Opens Up About ADHD Struggles: A Teacher Told Me 'I'd Never Amount to Anything,'" *People,* April 28, 2017, Accessed May 10, 2024. https://people.com/sports/michael-phelps-opens-up-about-adhd-struggles-in-new-video-a-teacher-told-me-id-never-amount-to-anything/

10   Nerenberg, Jenara, "When Adult ADHD Looks Something Like 'Flow,'" *The Cut,* July 6, 2026, Accessed May 10, 2024. https://www.thecut.com/2016/07/when-adult-adhd-looks-something-like-flow.html

11   Mandel, Howie, "I Have A Tough Time Being Myself," ADDitude, March 10, 2022, Accessed May 10, 2024. https://www.additudemag.com/howie-mandel-ocd/

12   Steed, Les, "The Night Watchman Theory for ADHD," ADD*itude*, October 11, 2023, Accessed May 10, 2024. https://www.additudemag.com/watchman-theory-adhd/

13   Edge Foundation, "Jim Carrey—A Life in Color," EdgeFoundation.com, Accessed May 10, 2024. https://edgefoundation.org/jim-carrey-a-life-of-color/

14   Paris Hilton (@ParisHilton), "The only rule is don't be boring and dress cute wherever you go. Life is too short to blend in. xo Paris bit.ly/NfoORn," Twitter, August 10, 2012, 7:37 p.m., https://twitter.com/ParisHilton/status/234071117944467456

15   Levine, Adam, "Maroon 5's Adam Levine: 'ADHD Isn't a Bad Thing," ADD*itude*. December 4, 2019, Accessed May 10, 2024. https://www.additudemag.com/adam-levine-adhd-is-not-a-bad-thing-and-you-are-not-alone/

16   Krzyzewski, Mike, and Phillips, Donald T., *Leading with the Heart* (New York, NY: Grand Central Publishing, 2001), Print.

17   ABC News, "Simone Biles Addresses Leaked Medical Records and ADHD Misconceptions," ABC*News.com*, September 14, 2016, Accessed May 10, 2024. https://abcnews.go.com/Health/simone-biles-addresses-leaked-medical-records-adhd-misconceptions/story?id=42076596

18   Alex Forsythe, "Fred Rogers: Look for the Helpers," *Youtube* video, 0:57, April 15, 2013, https://www.youtube.com/watch?v=-LGHtc_D328

19   Perot, Ross, "Quotes," RossPerot.com, Accessed May 10, 2024. https://www.rossperot.com/quotes-and-books

20   SpaceX (@SpaceX), "Congratulations to the entire SpaceX team on an exciting first integrated flight test of Starship!," Twitter, April 20, 2023, 9:44 p.m., https://twitter.com/SpaceX/status/1649046480144191489

21   60 Minutes, "2012: SpaceX: Elon Musk's race to space," *Youtube* video, 14:35, December 9, 2018, https://www.youtube.com/watch?v=23GzpbNUyI4

22   Roggli, Linda, "Entrepreneurship and ADHD: Fast Brain, Fast Company?,"*ADDitude.com*, June 15, 2022, Accessed May 10, 2024. https://www.additudemag.com/entrepreneurship-adhd-business-research-traits-stories/#:~:text=ADHD%20entrepreneurs%20think%20fast%2C%20talk,%E2%80%9D%20says%20Johan%20Wiklund%2C%20Ph

23   Roggli, Linda, "Entrepreneurship and ADHD: Fast Brain, Fast Company?,"*ADDitude.com*, June 15, 2022, Accessed May 10, 2024. https://www.additudemag.com/entrepreneurship-adhd-business-research-traits-stories/#:~:text=ADHD%20entrepreneurs%20think%20fast%2C%20talk,%E2%80%9D%20says%20Johan%20Wiklund%2C%20Ph

24   Deschanel, Zooey, "Crafternoon with Zooey D," *HelloGiggles.com*, June 2, 2011, Accessed May 10, 2024. http://web.archive.org/web/20150123080606/http:/hellogiggles.com/crafternoon-with-zooey-d

25   Simone Biles (@Simone_Biles), "I'd rather regret the risks that didn't work out than the chances I didn't take at all," Twitter, May 11, 2016, 12:37 a.m., https://twitter.com/Simone_Biles/status/730255395554365441?lang=en

26   Edge Foundation, "Was ADHD An Evolutionary Advantage?," *EdgeFoundation.com*, Accessed May 10, 2024. https://edgefoundation. org/was-adhd-an-evolutionary-advantage/,

27   Goldman, Laura, Robinson, Dana, and Krans, Brian, "ADHD and Evolution: Were Hyperactive Hunter-Gatherers Better Adapted Than Their Peers?," *Healthline.com*, March 15, 2021, Accessed May 10, 2024. https://www.healthline.com/health/adhd/evolution

28   Friedman, Richard A. "A Natural Fix for A.D.H.D.," *The New York Times*, October 31, 2014, Accessed May 10, 2024. https://www.nytimes. com/2014/11/02/opinion/sunday/a-natural-fix-for-adhd.html?_r=0

29   World Entertainment News Network, "Rodriguez Held Back By Attention Deficit Disorder," ContactMusic.com, June 19, 2006, Accessed May 10, 2024. https://www.contactmusic.com/michelle-rodriguez/ news/rodriguez-held-back-by-attention-deficit-disorder_100023

30   iFunny.com, Accessed May 10, 2024. https://ifunny.co/ picture/when-i-m-80-i-don-t-want-people-to-eeAy9ujJ9

31   Barkley, Russell, "How ADHD Affects Life Expectancy," *ADDitude. com*, September 20, 2022, Accessed May 10, 2024. https://www. additudemag.com/adhd-life-expectancy-video/#:~:text=ADHD%20 can%20reduce%20life%20expectancy,D.

32   Collins, Nancy, "Will Smith: Big Willie Style," *Rolling Stone*, December 10, 1998, Accessed May 10, 2024. https://www.rollingstone. com/tv-movies/tv-movie-news/will-smith-big-willie-style-202597/

33   Talk of the Nation, "The Myth of Multitasking,"NPR. *org*, May 10, 2013, Accessed May 10, 2024. https://www.npr. org/2013/05/10/182861382/the-myth-of-multitasking

34 Rotz, Roland, and Wright, Sarah D., "The Body-Brain Connection: How Fidgeting Sharpens Focus," *ADDitude.com*, February 15, 2024, Accessed May 10, 2024. https://www.additudemag.com/focus-factors/

35 Bonnie, Emily, "Addicted to Multitasking: The Scientific Reasons You Can't Stop Juggling Work," Wrike.com, July 28, 2021, Accessed May 10, 2024. https://www.wrike.com/blog/addicted-multitasking-scientific-reasons-you-cant-stop-juggling-work/

36 Forbes, Elizabeth, "Football Legend Terry Bradshaw's Fight Against ADD & Depression," HopeToCope.com, February 1, 2022, Accessed May 10, 2024. https://www.hopetocope.com/quaterback-scramble/

37 Thompson, Hunter S. "Hunter S. Thompson Quotes," *Goodreads.com*, Accessed May 10, 2024. https://www.goodreads.com/author/quotes/5237.Hunter_S_Thompson

38 Edwards, Natalie, "The Voice judge will.i.am tells of his battle with ADHD," *The Mirror*, April 28, 2013, Accessed May 10, 2024. https://www.mirror.co.uk/3am/celebrity-news/voice-judge-william-tells-battle-1857345

39 Diana, Princess of Wales, "Diana Princess of Wales Quotes," *Goodreads.com*, Accessed May 10, 2024. https://www.goodreads.com/author/quotes/2859627.Diana_Princess_of_Wales#:~:text=Everyone%20of%20us%20needs%20to,the%20process%2C%20care%20for%20ourselves.&text=I'd%20like%20to%20be,being%20queen%20of%20this%20country.&text=If%20you%20find%20someone%20you%20love%20in%20your%20life,hang%20on%20to%20that%20love

40   McCabe, Jessica, "This is what it's really like to live with ADHD," TED.com, July 2017, Accessed May 10, 2024. https://www.ted.com/talks/jessica_mccabe_this_is_what_it_s_really_like_to_live_with_adhd_jan_2017?language=en

41   Understood, "Dav Pilkey sees ADHD and Dyslexia as his superpowers," Understood.org, Accessed May 10, 2024. https://www.understood.org/en/articles/dav-pilkey-adhd-dyslexia-superpowers

42   Gostin, Nicki, "'Revolution' Host Ty Pennington Talks Lifelong Battle with ADHD," *Huffpost.com*, February 21, 2012, Accessed May 10, 2024. https://www.huffpost.com/entry/ty-pennington-the-revolution-adhd_n_1292059

43   Hamilton, Jeff, "Cammi Granato and ADHD: Female Role Model," *Psychology Today*, September 1, 2011, Accessed May 10, 2024. https://www.psychologytoday.com/us/blog/pills-dont-teach-skills/201109/cammi-granato-adhd-female-role-model

44   otally ADD, "Cycling, Exercising and ADHD—With Greg LeMond," *Totally ADD*, Accessed May 10, 2024. https://totallyadd.com/adhd-video/greg-lemond-cycling-and-exercising/

45   Hetrick, Adam, "Audrau McDonald Takes on Time Magazine Editor Following Accusatory ADHD Op-Ed," *Playbill*, June 11, 2014, Accessed May 10, 2024. https://playbill.com/article/audra-mcdonald-takes-on-time-magazine-editor-following-accusatory-adhd-op-ed-com-322387

46   Gilman, Lois, "How to Succeed in Business with ADHD," *ADDitude.com*, February 18, 2021, Accessed May 10, 2024. https://www.additudemag.com/adhd-entrepreneur-stories-jetblue-kinkos-jupitermedia/

47   Smith, Michelle R., "Army hat banned: Toy soldiers run afoul of school's weapons ban," *The Register Mail*, June 18, 2010, Accessed May 10, 2024. https://www.galesburg.com/story/news/2010/06/18/army-hat-banned-toy-soldiers/44367926007/

48   Kohl, Luke, "My Prison Without Bars," *ADDitude.com*, March 31, 2022, Accessed May 10, 2024. https://www.additudemag.com/my-prison-without-bars/

49   The Neurodiversity Charity ADHD Foundation (@ADHDFoundation), Celebrity Chef, Jamie Oliver, was diagnosed with ADHD in childhood. He manages his symptoms with a healthy diet #adhd," Twitter, October 31, 2014, 3:00 a.m., https://twitter.com/adhdfoundation/status/528079017799589888?lang=en

50   Bird, Natasha, "Emma Watson's Best Quotes of All Time,"*Elle*, April 15, 2016, Accessed May 10, 2024. https://www.elle.com/uk/life-and-culture/news/g30191/emma-watsons-best-quotes-of-all-time/?slide=1

51   Radar Staff, "The Real Reason Britney Spears Has Been Walking Off X Factor Set During Auditions," *Radar Online*, May 31,2012, Accessed May 10, 2024. https://radaronline.com/exclusives/2012/05/britney-spears-walking-x-factor-auditions-adhd/

52   Zemler, Emily, "Drugs, Despiration, and Dementia: 'Britney vs. Spears' Reveals New Horrors in Conservatorship," Rolling Stone, September 28, 2021, Accessed May 10, 2024. https://www.rollingstone.com/music/music-news/britney-vs-spears-things-we-learned-1232932/